Mary Wortley Lady Montagu

Letters of the Right Honourable Lady M-y W-y M-e:

Written During her Travels in Europe, Asia, and Africa. Vol. I

Mary Wortley Lady Montagu

Letters of the Right Honourable Lady M-y W-y M-e:
Written During her Travels in Europe, Asia, and Africa. Vol. I

ISBN/EAN: 9783744722094

Printed in Europe, USA, Canada, Australia, Japan

Cover: Foto ©Andreas Hilbeck / pixelio.de

More available books at **www.hansebooks.com**

LETTERS

OF THE RIGHT HONOURABLE

Lady M—y W——y M——e:

Written during her TRAVELS in

EUROPE, ASIA, AND AFRICA,

TO

Perſons of Diſtinction, Men of Letters, &c. in different Parts of EUROPE.

WHICH CONTAIN

AMONG OTHER CURIOUS RELATIONS,

Accounts of the POLICY and MANNERS of the TURKS;

Drawn from Sources that have been inacceſſible to other Travellers.

A NEW EDITION.

To which are now firſt added,

P O E M S,

By the ſame AUTHOR.

IN TWO VOLUMES.

VOL. I.

LONDON:

Printed for T. CADELL, and T. EVANS, in the Strand; J. MURRAY, in Fleet-Street; and R. BALDWIN, in Pater-noſter-Row.

MDCCLXXXIV.

PREFACE

BY A

LADY.

Written in 1724.

I WAS going, like common editors, to advertise the reader of the beauties and excellencies of the work laid before him: To tell him that the illustrious author had opportunities, that other travellers, whatever their quality or curiosity may have been, cannot obtain; and a genius capable of making the best improvement of every opportunity.

But if the reader after perusing *one* letter only, has not discernment to distinguish that natural elegance, that delicacy of sentiment and observation, that easy gracefulness, and lovely simplicity (which is the perfection of writing) and in which these

PREFACE.

these Letters exceed all that has appeared in this kind, or almost in any other, let him lay the book down, and leave it to those who have.

The noble author had the goodness to lend me her MS. to satisfy my curiosity in some enquiries I had made concerning her travels; and when I had it in my hands, how was it possible to part with it? I once had the vanity to hope I might acquaint the public, that it owed this invaluable treasure to my importunities. But alas! the most ingenious author has condemned it to obscurity during her life; and conviction, as well as deference, obliges me to yield to her reasons. However, if these Letters appear hereafter when I am in my grave, let this attend them, in testimony to posterity, that among her cotemporaries, *one* woman, at least, was just to her merit.

There is not any thing so excellent, but some will carp at it, and the rather, because of its excellency. But to such hypercritics, I shall only say * * * * * *
* * * * * * * * * * * * * *
I confess,

PREFACE.

I confess, I am malicious enough to desire, that the world should see, to how much better purpose the LADIES travel than their LORDS; and that, whilst it is surfeited with *Male Travels*, all in the same tone, and stuft with the same trifles; a lady has the skill to strike out a new path, and to embellish a worn-out subject, with variety of fresh and elegant entertainment. For besides the vivacity and spirit which enlivens every part, and that inimitable beauty which spreads through the whole; besides the purity of the style, for which it may be justly accounted the standard of the English tongue; the reader will find a more true and accurate account of the customs and manners of the several nations, with whom this lady conversed, than he can in any other author. But as her ladyship's penetration discovers the inmost follies of the heart, so the candour of her temper passed over them with an air of pity rather than reproach; treating with the politeness of a court, and the gentleness of a lady, what the severity of her judgment could not but condemn.

PREFACE.

genius, as I do in the sincerity of my soul, pleased that a *woman* triumphs, and proud to follow in her train. Let us offer her the palm which is so justly her due; and if we pretend to any laurels, lay them willingly at her feet.

December 18, 1724.   M. A.

Charm'd into love of what obscures my fame,
If I had wit, I'd celebrate her name,
And all the beauties of her mind proclaim.
Till Malice, deafen'd with the mighty sound,
It's ill-concerted calumnies confound;
Let fall the mask, and with pale Envy meet,
To ask, and find, their pardon at her feet.

You see, Madam, how I lay every thing at your feet. As the tautology shews the poverty of my genius, it likewise shews the extent of your empire over my imagination.

May 31, 1725.

LETTER I.

To the Countess of ———.

Rotterdam, Aug. 3, O.S. 1716.

I FLATTER myself (dear sister) that I shall give you some pleasure in letting you know that I have safely passed the sea, though we had the ill fortune of a storm. We were persuaded by the captain of the yacht to set out in a calm, and he pretended there was nothing so easy as to tide it over; but, after two days slowly moving, the wind blew so hard, that none of the sailors could keep their feet, and we were all Sunday night tossed very handsomely. I never saw a man more frighted than the captain. For my part, I have been so lucky, neither to suffer from fear nor sea-sickness; tho', I confess, I was so impatient to see myself once more upon dry land, that I would not stay till the yacht could get to Rotterdam, but went in the longboat to Helvoetsluys, where we had voitures to carry us to the Briel. I was charmed with the neatness of that little town; but my arrival at Rotterdam presented me a new scene of pleasure. All the streets are paved with broad stones, and before many of the meanest artificers doors are placed seats of various-coloured marbles, so neatly kept, that I assure you, I walked almost all over the town yesterday, incognito, in my slippers, without receiving one spot of dirt; and you may see the Dutch maids washing the pavement of the street with more application than ours do our bed chambers. The town seems so full of people, with such busy faces, all in motion, that I can hardly fancy it is not some celebrated fair; but I see it is every day the same. 'Tis certain no town can be more advantageously situated for commerce. Here are seven large canals, on which the merchant ships come up to the very doors of their houses. The shops and warehouses are of a surprizing neatness and magnificence, filled with an incredible quantity of fine merchandize, and so much cheaper than

what

what we see in England, that I have much ado to persuade myself I am still so near it. Here is neither dirt nor beggary to be seen. One is not shock'd with those loathsome cripples, so common in London, nor teized with the importunity of idle fellows and wenches, that chuse to be nasty and lazy. The common servants and little shop-women, here, are more nicely clean, than most of our ladies, and the great variety of neat dresses (every woman dressing her head after her own fashion) is an additional pleasure in seeing the town. You see, hitherto, I make no complaints, dear sister, and if I continue to like travelling as well as I do at present, I shall not repent my project. It will go a great way in making me satisfied with it, if it affords me an opportunity of entertaining you. But it is not from Holland, that you must expect a disinterested offer. I can write enough in the stile of Rotterdam, to tell you plainly, in one word, that I expect returns of all the London news. You see I have already learnt to make a good bargain, and that it is not for nothing I will so much as tell you, I am, your affectionate sister.

LETTER II.

To Mrs. S.——

Hague, Aug. 5, O.S. 1716.

I MAKE haste to tell you, dear Madam, that after all the dreadful fatigues you threatened me with, I am hitherto very well pleased with my journey. We take care to make such short stages every day, that I rather fancy myself upon parties of pleasure, than upon the road; and sure nothing can be more agreeable than travelling in Holland. The whole country appears a large garden; the roads are well paved, shaded on each side with rows of trees, and bordered with large canals, full of boats, passing and repassing. Every twenty paces gives you the prospect of some villa, and every four hours, that of a large town, so surprizingly neat, I am sure you would be charmed with them. The place I

am

am now at, is certainly one of the finest villages in the world. Here are several squares finely built, and (what I think a particular beauty) the whole set with thick large trees. The Voor-hout is, at the same time, the Hyde Park and Mall of the people of quality; for they take the air in it both on foot and in coaches. There are shops for wafers, cool liquors, &c. I have been to see several of the most celebrated gardens, but I will not teize you with their descriptions. I dare swear you thing my letter already long enough. But I must not conclude without begging your pardon, for not obeying your commands, in sending the lace you ordered me. Upon my word I can yet find none, that is not dearer than you may buy it in London. If you want any India goods, here are great variety of penny-worths, and I shall follow your orders with great pleasure and exactness, being,

    Dear, Madam, &c. &c.

LETTER III.

To Mrs. S. C.

Nimeguen, Aug. 13, O. S. 1716.

I AM extremely sorry, my dear S. that your fears of disobliging your relations, and their fears for your health and safety, have hindered me from enjoying the happiness of your company, and you the pleasure of a diverting journey. I receive some degree of mortification from every agreeable novelty, or pleasing prospect, by the reflection of your having so unluckily missed the delight which I know it would have given you. If you were with me in this town, you would be ready to expect to receive visits from your Nottingham friends. No two places were ever more resembling; one has but to give the Maese the name of the Trent, and there is no distinguishing the prospect. The houses, like those of Nottingham are built one above another, and are intermixed, in the

the same manner, with trees and gardens. The Tower, they call Julius Cæsar's, has the same situation with Nottingham Castle; and I cannot help fancying I see from it the Trent-field, Adboulton, places so well known to us. 'Tis true, the fortifications make a considerable difference. All the learned in the art of war, bestow great commendations on them; for my part, that know nothing of the matter, I shall content myself with telling you, 'tis a very pretty walk on the ramparts, on which there is a tower, very deservedly called the Belvidera, where people go to drink coffee, tea, &c. and enjoy one of the finest prospects in the world. The public walks have no great beauty, but the thick shade of the trees, which is solemnly delightful. But I must not forget to take notice of the bridge, which appeared very surprising to me. It is large enough to hold hundreds of men, with horses and carriages. They give the value of an English two-pence to get upon it, and then away they go, bridge and all, to the other side of the river, with so slow a motion, one is hardly sensible of any at all. I was yesterday at the French church, and stared very much at their manner of service. The parson clapped on a broad-brimmed hat in the first place, which gave him entirely the air of, what d'ye call him, in Bartholomew fair, which he kept up by extraordinary antic gestures, and preaching much such stuff, as t'other talked to the puppets. However, the congregation seemed to receive it with great devotion; and I was informed by some of his flock, that he is a person of particular fame amongst them. I believe, by this time, you are as much tired with my account of him, as I was with his sermon; but I am sure your brother will excuse a digression in favour of the church of England. You know, speaking disrespectfully of the Calvinists, is the same thing as speaking honourably of the church. Adieu, my dear S. always remember me, and be assured, I can never forget you, &c. &c.

LETTER IV.

To the Lady ————.

Cologn, Aug. 16, O.S. 1716.

IF my lady ———— could have any notions of the fatigues that I have suffered these two last days, I am sure she would own it a great proof of regard, that I now sit down to write to her. We hired horses from Nimeguen hither, not having the conveniency of the post, and found but very indifferent accommodations at Reinberg, our first stage; but it was nothing to what I suffered yesterday. We were in hopes to reach Cologn; our horses tired at Stamel, three hours from it, where I was forced to pass the night in my clothes, in a room not at all better than a hovel; for though I have my bed with me, I had no mind to undress, where the wind came from a thousand places. We left this wretched lodging at daybreak, and about six this morning came safe here,

here, where I got immediately into bed. I slept so well for three hours, that I found myself perfectly recovered, and have had spirits enough to go and see all that is curious in the town, that is to say, the churches, for here is nothing else worth seeing. This is a very large town, but the most part of it is old built. The Jesuits' church, which is the neatest, was shewed me, in a very complaisant manner, by a handsome young Jesuit; who, not knowing who I was, took a liberty in his compliments and railleries, which very much diverted me. Having never before seen any thing of that nature, I could not enough admire the magnificence of the altars, the rich images of the saints, (all massy silver) and the enchasures of the relicks, tho' I could not help murmuring in my heart, at the profusion of pearls, diamonds, and rubies, bestowed on the adornment of rotten teeth and dirty rags. I own that I had wickedness enough to covet St. Ursula's pearl necklace; though perhaps this was no wickedness at all,— an image not being certainly one's neighbour;

but

but I went yet further, and wished the wench herself converted into dressing plate. I should also gladly see converted into silver, a great St. Christopher, which I imagine would look very well in a cistern. These were my pious reflections; though I was very well satisfied to see, piled up to the honour of our nation, the skulls of the Eleven Thousand Virgins. I have seen some hundreds of relics here, of no less consequence; but I will not imitate the common stile of travellers so far, as to give you a list of them, being persuaded that you have no manner of curiosity for the titles given to jawbones, and bits of worm-eaten wood.—Adieu. I am just going to supper, where I shall drink your health in an admirable sort of Lorrain wine, which I am sure is the same you call Burgundy in London, &c. &c.

LETTER V.

To the Countess of B——.

Nuremberg, Aug. 22, O.S. 1716.

AFTER five days travelling post, I could not sit down to write on any other occasion than to tell my dear Lady, that I have not forgot her obliging command of sending her some account of my travels. I have already passed a large part of Germany, have seen all that is remarkable in Cologn, Frankfort, Wurtsburg, and this place. 'Tis impossible not to observe the difference between the free towns, and those under the government of absolute princes, as all the little sovereigns of Germany are. In the first there appears an air of commerce and plenty. The streets are well built, and full of people, neatly and plainly dressed. The shops are loaded with merchandize, and the commonalty are clean and chearful.---- In the other you see a sort of shabby finery, a numa number of dirty people of quality tawdered out; narrow nasty streets out of repair, wretchedly thin of inhabitants, and above half of the common sort asking alms. I cannot help fancying one, under the figure of a clean Dutch citizen's wife, and the other like a poor town lady of pleasure, painted, and ribboned out in her head-dress, with tarnished silver-laced shoes, a ragged under-petticoat, a miserable mixture of vice and poverty. —They have sumptuary laws in this town, which distinguish their rank by their dress, prevent the excess which ruins so many other cities, and has a more agreeable effect to the eye of a stranger, than our fashions. I need not be ashamed to own, that I wish these laws were in force in other parts of the world. When one considers impartially, the merit of a rich suit of clothes in most places, the respect and the smiles of favour it procures, not to speak of the envy and the sighs it occasions (which is very often the principal charm to the wearer) one is forced to confess, that there is need of an uncommon understanding, to resist the temptation of pleasing friends,

friends and mortifying rivals; and that it is natural to young people to fall into a folly, which betrays them to that want of money, which is the source of a thousand basenesses. What numbers of men have begun the world with generous inclinations, that have afterwards been the instruments of bringing misery on a whole people, being led by a vain expence into debts that they could clear no other way, but by the forfeit of their honour, and which they never could have contracted, if the respect the multitude pays to habits, was fixed by law, only to a particular colour or cut of plain cloth. These reflections draw after them others that are too melancholy. I will make haste to put them out of your head by the farce of relicks, with which I have been entertained in all Romish churches.

The Lutherans are not quite free from these follies. I have seen here in the principal church, a large piece of the Cross set in jewels, and the point of the spear, which, they told me, very gravely, was the same that pierced the side

of

of our Saviour. But I was particularly diverted in a little Roman catholic church, which is permitted here, where the profeſſors of that religion are not very rich, and conſequently cannot adorn their images in ſo rich a manner as their neighbours: For not to be quite deſtitute of all finery, they have dreſſed up an image of our Saviour over the altar, in a fair full bottomed wig, very well powdered. I imagine I ſee your ladyſhip ſtare at this article, of which you very much doubt the veracity: but, upon my word, I have not yet made uſe of the priviledge of a traveller, and my whole account is written with the ſame plain ſincerity of heart, with which I aſſure you that I am, dear Madam,

Yours, &c. &c.

LETTER VI.

To Mrs. P————

Ratisbon, Aug. 30, O.S. 1716,

I HAD the pleasure of receiving yours but the day before I left London. I give you a thousand thanks for your good wishes, and have such an opinion of their efficacy, that I am persuaded, I owe, in part to them the good luck of having proceeded so far on my long journey without any ill accident. For I don't reckon it any to have been stopped a few days, in this town, by a cold, since it has not only given me an opportunity of seeing all that is curious in it, but of making some acquaintance with the ladies, who have all been to see me with great civility, particularly Madame ————, the wife of our King's envoy from Hanover. She has carried me to all the assemblies, and I have been magnificently entertained at her house, which is one of the finest

finest here. You know that all the nobility of this place are Envoys from different States. Here are a great number of them, and they might pass their time agreeably enough, if they were less delicate on the point of ceremony. But instead of joining in the design of making the town as pleasant to one another as they can, and improving their little societies, they amuse themselves no other way, than with perpetual quarrels, which they take care to eternize, by leaving them to their successors; and an Envoy to Ratisbon receives, regularly, half a dozen quarrels, among the perquisites of his employment. You may be sure the ladies are not wanting, on their side, in cherishing and improving those important piques, which divide the town almost into as many parties, as there are families. They chuse rather to suffer the mortification of sitting almost alone on their assembly nights, than to recede one jot from their pretensions. I have not been here above a week, and yet I have heard from almost every one of them, the whole history of their wrongs, and dreadful com-

complaints of the injustice of their neighbours, in hopes to draw me to their party. But I think it very prudent to remain neuter, though if I was to stay amongst them, there would be no possibility of continuing so, their quarrels running so high, that they will not be civil to those that visit their adversaries. The foundation of these everlasting disputes, turns entirely upon rank, place, and the title of Excellency, which they all pretend to, and what is very hard, will give it to no body. For my part I could not forbear advising them (for the public good) to give the title of Excellency to every body, which would include the receiving it from every body; but the very mention of such a dishonourable peace, was received with as much indignation, as Mrs. Blackaire did the motion of a reference. And indeed, I began to think myself ill-natured, to offer to take from them, in a town where there are so few diversions, so entertaining an amusement. I know that my peaceable disposition already gives me a very ill figure, and that 'tis pub-

publickly whispered as a piece of impertinent pride in me, that I have hitherto been saucily civil to every body, as if I thought no body good enough to quarrel with. I should be obliged to change my behaviour, if I did not intend to pursue my journey in a few days. I have been to see the churches here, and had the permission of touching the relicks, which was never suffered in places where I was not known. I had, by this privilege, an opportunity of making an observation, which I doubt not, might have been made in all the other churches, that the emeralds and rubies which they shew round their relicks and images, are most of them false; though they tell you that many of the Crosses and Madonas set round with these stones, have been the gifts of Emperors, and other great Princes. I don't doubt indeed but they were at first jewels of value; but the good fathers have found it convenient to apply them to other uses, and the people are just as well satisfied with bits of glass amongst these relicks. They shewed me a prodigious claw set in gold, which they called

the

the claw of a griffin; and I could not forbear asking the Reverend Priest that shewed it, whether the Griffin was a Saint? The question almost put him beside his gravity; but he answered, they only kept it as a curiosity. I was very much scandalized at a large silver image of the Trinity, where the Father is represented under the figure of a decrepit old man, with a beard down to his knees, and tripple crown upon his head, holding in his arms the Son, fixed on the Cross, and the Holy Ghost, in the shape of a dove, hovering over him. Madam——is come this minute to call me to the assembly, and forces me to tell you very abruptly, that I am ever your, &c. &c.

LETTER VII.

To the Countess of ————

Vienna, Sept. 8, O. S. 1716.

I AM now, my dear sister, safely arrived at Vienna, and I thank God, have not at all suffered in my health, nor (what is dearer to me) in that of my child, by all our fatigues. We travelled by water from Ratisbon, a journey perfectly agreeable, down the Danube, in one of those little vessels, that they, very properly, call wooden houses, having in them all the conveniences of a palace, stoves in the chambers, kitchens, &c. they are rowed by twelve men each, and with such incredible swiftness, that in the same day you have the pleasure of a vast variety of prospects, and within the space of a few hours you have the pleasure of seeing a populous city, adorned with magnificent palaces, and the most romantic solitudes, which appear distant from the commerce of mankind, the banks of the

Danube

Danube being charmingly diversified with woods, rocks, mountains covered with vines, fields of corn, large cities and ruins of ancient castles. I saw the great towns of Passau and Lintz, famous for the retreat of the Imperial Court, when Vienna was besieged. This town, which has the honour of being the Emperor's residence, did not at all answer my expectation, nor ideas of it, being much less than I expected to find it; the streets are very close, and so narrow, one cannot observe the fine fronts of the palaces, though many of them very well deserve observation, being truly magnificent. They are all built of fine white stone, and are excessive high. For as the town is too little for the number of the people that desire to live in it, the builders seem to have projected to repair that misfortune, by clapping one town on the top of another, most of the houses being of five, and some of them six stories. You may easily imagine that, the streets being so narrow, the rooms are extremely dark, and what is an inconveniency

veniency much more intolerable in my opinion, there is no house has so few as five or six families in it. The apartments of the greatest ladies, and even of the ministers of state, are divided, but by a partition, from that of a taylor or shoe-maker, and I know no body that has above two floors in any house, one for their own use, and one higher for their servants. Those that have houses of their own let out the rest of them, to whoever will take them, and thus the great stairs (which are all of stone) are as common and as dirty as the street. 'Tis true, when you have once travelled through them, nothing can be more surprizingly magnificent than the apartments. They are commonly a suite of eight or ten large rooms, all inlaid, the doors and windows richly carved and gilt, and the furniture such as is seldom seen in the palaces of sovereign princes in other countries. Their apartments are adorned with hangings of the finest tapestry of Brussels, prodigious large looking glasses in silver frames, fine japan tables, beds, chairs, canopies, and window curtains of the richeſt Genoa damaſk or velvet, almoſt covered with gold lace or embroidery. All this is made gay by pictures and vaſt jars of japan china, and large luſtres of rock cryſtal. I have already had the honour of being invited to dinner by ſeveral of the firſt people of quality, and I muſt do them the juſtice to ſay, the good taſte and magnificence of their tables very well anſwer to that of their furniture. I have been more than once entertained with different diſhes of meat, all ſerved in ſilver, and well dreſſed, the deſert proportionable, ſerved in the fineſt china. But the variety and richneſs of their wines, is what appears the moſt ſurprizing. The conſtant way is, to lay a liſt of their names upon the plates of the gueſts along with the napkins, and I have counted ſevèral times, to the number of eighteen different ſorts, all exquiſite in their kinds. I was yeſterday at Count Schoonbourn, the

Vice-

Vice-chancellor's garden, where I was invited to dinner. I muſt own, I never ſaw a place ſo perfectly delightful as the Fauxbourg of Vienna. It is very large, and almoſt wholly compoſed of delicious palaces. If the Emperor found it proper to permit the gates of the town to be laid open, that the Fauxbourgs might be joined to it, he would have one of the largeſt and beſt built cities in Europe. Count Schoonbourn's villa is one of the moſt magnificent; the furniture all rich brocades, ſo well fancied and fitted up, nothing can look more gay and ſplendid; not to ſpeak of a gallery full of rarities of coral, mother of pearl, and throughout the whole houſe a profuſion of gilding, carving, fine paintings, the moſt beautiful porcelain, ſtatues of alabaſter and ivory, and vaſt orange and lemon trees in gilt pots. The dinner was perfectly fine and well ordered, and made ſtill more agreeable by the good-humour of the Count. I have not yet been at court, being forced to ſtay for my
gown,

gown, without which there is no waiting on the Emprefs; though I am not without great impatience to fee a beauty that has been the admiration of fo many different nations. When I have had that honour, I will not fail to let you know my real thoughts, always taking a particular pleafure in communicating them to my dear fifter.

LETTER VIII.

To Mr. P——.

Vienna, Sept. 14; O.S

PERHAPS you'll laugh at me, for thanking you very gravely for all the obliging concern you expreſs for me. 'Tis certain that I may, if I pleaſe, take the fine things you ſay to me for wit and raillery, and it may be, it would be taking them right. But I never, in my life, was half ſo well diſpoſed to take you in earneſt, as I am at preſent, and that diſtance which makes the continuation of your friendſhip improbable, has very much increaſed my faith in it. I find that I have (as well as the reſt of my ſex) whatever face I ſet on't, a ſtrong diſpoſition to believe in miracles. Don't fancy, however, that I am infected by the air of theſe popiſh countries; I have, indeed, ſo far wandered from the diſcipline of the church of England, as to have been laſt Sunday at the opera, which was performed in the garden of the Favorita,

Favorita, and I was so much pleased with it, I have not yet repented my seeing it. Nothing of that kind ever was more magnificent; and I can easily believe, what I am told, that the decorations and habits cost the Emperor thirty thousand pounds sterling. The stage was built over a very large canal, and at the beginning of the second act, divided into two parts, discovering the water, on which there immediately came from different parts, two fleets of little gilded vessels, that gave the representation of a naval fight. It is not easy to imagine the beauty of this scene, which I took particular notice of. But all the re were perfectly fine in their kind. The story of the opera was the Enchantment of Alcina, which gives opportunities for great variety of machines and changes of the scenes, which are performed with a surprizing swiftness. The theatre is so large that 'tis hard to carry the eye to the end of it, and the habits in the utmost magnificence to the number of one hundred and eight. No house could hold such large decorations; but

but the ladies all fitting in the open air, expofes them to great inconveniences; for there is but one canopy for the imperial family; and the firft night it was reprefented, a heavy fhower of rain happening, the opera was broke off, and the company crouded away in fuch confufion, that I was almoft fqueezed to death.—But if their operas are thus delightful, their comedies are in as high a degree ridiculous. They had but one play-houfe, where I had the curiofity to go to a German comedy, and was very glad it happened to be the ftory of Amphitrion. As that fubject has been already handled by a Latin, French, and Englifh poet, I was curious to fee what an Auftrian author would make of it. I underftood enough of that language to comprehend the greateft part of it, and befides I took with me a lady that had the goodnefs to explain to me every word. The way is to take a box which holds four, for yourfelf and company. The fixed price is a gold ducat. I thought the houfe very low and dark; but I confefs the comedy
admirably

admirably recompenfed that defect. I never laughed fo much in my life. It begun with Jupiter's falling in love out of a peep-hole in the clouds, and ended with the birth of Hercules. But what was moſt pleafant was the ufe Jupiter made of his metamorphofis, for you no fooner faw him under the figure of Amphitrion, but inſtead of flying to Alcmena, with the raptures Mr. Dryden puts into his mouth, he fends for Amphitrion's taylor, and cheats him of a laced coat, and his banker of a bag of money, a jew of a diamond ring, and befpeaks a great fupper in his name; and the greateſt part of the comedy turns upon poor Amphi-, trion's being tormented by thefe people for their debts. Mercury ufes Sofia in the fame manner. But I could not eafily pardon the liberty the poet has taken of larding his play with, not only indecent expreffions, but fuch grofs words as I don't think our mob would fuffer from a mountebank. Befides, the two Sofias very fairly let down their breeches in the direct view of the boxes, which were full

of

of people of the firſt rank, that ſeemed very well pleaſed with their entertainment, and aſſured me this was a celebrated piece. I ſhall conclude my letter with this remarkable relation, very well worthy the ſerious conſideration of Mr. Collier. I won't trouble you with farewell compliments, which I think generally as impertinent, as curtſies at leaving the room when the viſit had been too long already.

LETTER IX.

To the Countess of ———

Vienna, Sept. 14, O. S.

THOUGH I have so lately troubled you, my dear sister, with a long letter, yet I will keep my promise in giving you an account of my first going to court. In order to that ceremony, I was squeezed up in a gown, and adorned with a gorget and the other implements thereunto belonging, a dress very inconvenient, but which certainly shows the neck and shape to great advantage. I cannot forbear giving you some description of the fashions here, which are more monstrous and contrary to all common sense and reason, than 'tis possible for you to imagine. They build certain fabrics of gauze on their heads, about a yard high, consisting of three or four stories, fortified with numberless yards of heavy ribbon.

bon. The foundation of this structure is a thing they call a Bourlé, which is exactly of the same shape and kind, but about four times as big as those rolls our prudent milk-maids make use of to fix their pails upon. This machine they cover with their own hair, which they mix with a great deal of false, it being a particular beauty to have their heads too large to go into a moderate tub. Their hair is prodigiously powdered to conceal the mixture, and set out with three or four rows of bodkins (wonderfully large, that stick out two or three inches from their hair) made of diamonds, pearls, red, green, and yellow stones, that it certainly requires as much art and experience to carry the load upright, as to dance upon May-day with the garland. Their whalebone petticoats outdo ours by several yards circumference, and cover some acres of ground. You may easily suppose how this extraordinary dress sets off and improves the natural ugliness, with which God Almighty has been pleased to endow them, generally speaking. Even the lovely

lovely. Empress herself is obliged to comply, in some degree, with these absurd fashions, which they would not quit for all the world. I had a private audience (according to ceremony) of half an hour, and then all the other ladies were permitted to come and make their court. I was perfectly charmed with the Empress; I cannot however tell you that her features are regular; her eyes are not large, but have a lively look full of sweetness; her complexion the finest I ever saw; her nose and forehead well made, but her mouth has ten thousand charms, that touch the soul. When she smiles, 'tis with a beauty and sweetness, that forces adoration. She has a vast quantity of fine fair hair; but then her person!—one must speak of it poetically to do it rigid justice; all that the poets have said of the mien of Juno, the air of Venus, come not up to the truth. The Graces move with her; the famous statue of Medicis was not formed with more delicate proportions; nothing can be added to the beauty of her neck and hands. Till

I saw

I saw them, I did not believe there were any in nature so perfect, and I was almost sorry that my rank here did not permit me to kiss them; but they are kissed sufficiently, for every body that waits on her, pays that homage at their entrance, and when they take leave. When the ladies were come in, she sat down to *Quinze*. I could not play at a game I had never seen before, and she ordered me a seat at her right hand, and had the goodness to talk to me very much, with that grace so natural to her. I expected every moment, when the men were to come in to pay their court; but this drawing room is very different from that of England; no man enters it but the grand master, who comes in to advertise the Empress of the approach of the Emperor. His Imperial Majesty did me the honour of speaking to me in a very obliging manner, but he never speaks to any of the other ladies, and the whole passes with a gravity and air of ceremony that has something very formal in it. The Empress Amelia, dowager of the late Emperor Joseph,

Joseph, came this evening to wait on the reigning Empress, followed by the two archduchesses her daughters, who were very agreeable young Princesses. Their Imperial Majesties rose and went to meet her at the door of the room, after which she was seated in an armed chair next the Empress, and in the same manner at supper, and there the men had the permission of paying their court. The archduchesses sat on chairs with backs without arms. The table was entirely served and all the dishes set on by the Empress's maids of honour, which are twelve young ladies of the first quality. They have no salary, but their chamber at court, where they live in a sort of confinement, not being suffered to go to the assemblies or public places in town, except in compliment to the wedding of a sister maid, whom the Empress always presents with her picture set in diamonds. The three first of them are called Ladies of the Key, and wear gold keys by their sides; but what I find most pleasant, is the custom, which obliges them as long as they

they live, after they have left the Emprefs's service, to make her some present every year on the day of her feast. Her Majesty is served by no married women but the Grande Maitresse, who is generally a widow of the first quality, always very old, and is at the same time Groom of the Stole and mother of the maids. The dressers are not, at all, in the figure they pretend to in England, being looked upon no otherwise than as downright chamber-maids. I had an audience next day of the Emprefs mother, a princess of great virtue and goodness, but who piques herself too much on a violent devotion. She is perpetually performing extraordinary acts of penance, without having ever done any thing to deserve them. She has the same number of maids of honour, whom she suffers to go in colours; but she herself never quits her mourning; and sure nothing can be more dismal than the mourning here, even for a brother. There is not the least bit of linen to be seen; all black crape instead of it. The neck, ears, and side of the face are covered with

with a plaited piece of the same stuff, and the face that peeps out in the midst of it, looks as if it were pilloried. The widows wear, over and above, a crape fore-head cloth, and in this solemn weed, go to all the public places of diversion without scruple. The next day I was to wait on the Empress Amelia, who is now at her palace of retirement, half a mile from the town. I had there the pleasure of seeing a diversion wholly new to me, but which is the common amusement of this court. The Empress herself was seated on a little throne at the end of the fine alley in the garden, and on each side of her were ranged two parties of her ladies of quality, headed by two young arch-duchesses, all dressed in their hair, full of jewels, with fine light guns in their hands, and at proper distances were placed three oval pictures, which were the marks to be shot at. The first was that of a CUPID, filling a bumper of Burgundy, and the motto, "'Tis easy to be valiant here." The second a FORTUNE holding a garland in her hand, the motto,

motto, " For her whom Fortune favours." The third was a SWORD with a laurel wreath on the point, the motto, " Here is no shame " to the vanquished."—Near the Empress was a gilded trophy wreathed with flowers, and made of little crooks, on which were hung rich Turkish handkerchiefs, tippets, ribbons, laces, &c. for the small prizes. The Empress gave the first with her own hand, which was a fine ruby ring set round with diamonds in a gold snuff-box. There was for the second, a little Cupid set with brilliants, and besides these a set of fine china for the tea-table, enchased in gold, japan trunks, fans, and many gallantries of the same nature. All the men of quality at Vienna were spectators; but the ladies only had permission to shoot, and the arch-duchess Amelia carried off the first prize. I was very well pleased with having seen this entertainment, and I do not know but it might make as good a figure as the prize shooting in the Æneid, if I could write as well as Virgil. This is the favourite pleasure of the Emperor, and there is rarely a week without ſome feaſt of this kind, which makes the young ladies ſkilful enough to defend a fort. They laughed very much to ſee me afraid to handle a gun. My dear ſiſter, you will eaſily pardon an abrupt concluſion. I believe by this time you are ready to think I ſhall never conclude at all.

LETTER X.

To the Lady R ———.

Vienna, Sept. 20, 1716. O. S.

I AM extremely rejoiced, but not at all furprifed, at the long, delightful letter, you have had the goodnefs to fend me. I know that you can think of an abfent friend even in the midſt of a court, and you love to oblige, where you can have no view of a return, and I expect from you that you fhould love me, and think of me, when you don't fee me. I have compaffion for the mortifications, that you tell me befall our little, old friend, and I pity her much more, fince I know, that they are only owing to the barbarous cuftoms of our country. Upon my word, if fhe were here, fhe would have no other fault but that of being fomething too young for the fafhion, and fhe has nothing to do but to tranfplant herfelf hither about feven years hence, to be again a
young

young and blooming beauty. I can assure you that wrinkles, or a small stoop in the shoulders, nay even grey hairs, are no objection to the making new conquests. I know you cannot easily figure to yourself, a young fellow of five and twenty, ogling my Lady S-ff-k with passion, or pressing to hand the Countess of O———d from an Opera. But such are the sights I see every day, and I don't perceive any body surprized at them but myself. A woman, till five and thirty, is only looked upon as a raw girl, and can possibly make no noise in the world till about forty. I don't know what your ladyship may think of this matter, but 'tis a considerable comfort to me to know there is upon earth such a paradise for old women, and I am content to be insignificant at present, in the design of returning when I am fit to appear no where else. I cannot help lamenting on this occasion, the pitiful case of too many English ladies, long since retired to prudery and ratafia, who if their stars had luckily conducted hither, would still shine in

the

the first rank of beauties. Besides, that perplexing word reputation, has quite another meaning here than what you give it at London, and getting a lover, is so far from losing, that it is properly getting reputation; ladies being much more respected in regard to the rank of their lovers, than that of their husbands.

But what you will think very odd, the two sects that divide our whole nation of petticoats are utterly unknown in this place. Here are neither Coquettes nor Prudes. No woman dares appear coquette enough to encourage two lovers at a time. And I have not seen any such prudes, as to pretend fidelity to their husbands, who are certainly the best natured set of people in the world, and look upon their wives' gallants as favourably, as men do upon their deputies, that take the troublesome part of their business off their hands. They have not however the less to do on that account; for they are generally deputies in another place themselves; in one word 'tis the established custom

custom for every lady to have two husbands, one that bears the name, and another that performs the duties. And the engagements are so well known, that it would be a downright affront, and publickly resented, if you invited a woman of quality to dinner, without at the same time, inviting her two attendants of lover and husband, between whom she sits in state with great gravity. The sub-marriages generally last twenty years together, and the lady often commands the poor lover's estate, even to the utter ruin of his family. These connections, indeed, are as seldom begun by any real passion, as other matches; for a man makes but an ill figure that is not in some commerce of this nature, and a woman looks out for a lover as soon as she is married as part of her equipage, without which she could not be genteel, and the first article of the treaty is establishing the pension, which remains to the lady, in case the gallant should prove inconstant. This chargeable point of honour, I look upon as the real foundation of so many wonderful instances of constancy.

stancy. I really know several women of the first quality, whose pensions are as well known as their annual rents, and yet no body esteems them the less; on the contrary, their discretion would be called in question if they should be suspected to be mistresses for nothing. A great part of their emulation consists in trying who shall get most; and having no intrigue at all is so far a disgrace, that I'll assure you, a lady who is very much my friend here, told me but yesterday, how much I was obliged to her for justifying my conduct in a conversation relating to me, where it was publickly asserted, that I could not possibly have common sense, since I had been in town above a fortnight, and had made no steps towards commencing an amour. My friend pleaded for me, that my stay was uncertain, and she believed that was the cause of my seeming stupidity, and this was all she could find to say in my justification. But one of the pleasantest adventures I ever met in my life, was last night, and it will give you a just idea, in what a delicate manner the

Belles

Belles Passions are managed in this country. I was at the assembly of the Countess of ———, and the young Count of ——— leading me down stairs, asked me how long I was to stay at Vienna; I made answer that my stay depended on the Emperor, and it was not in my power to determine it. Well, Madam, (said he) whether your time here is to be longer or shorter, I think you ought to pass it agreeably, and to that end you must engage in a little affair of the heart.———My heart (answered I gravely enough) does not engage very easily, and I have no design of parting with it. I see, Madam, (said he sighing) by the ill nature of that answer, I am not to hope for it, which is a great mortification to me that am charmed with you. But, however, I am still devoted to your service, and since I am not worthy of entertaining you myself, do me the honour of letting me know, whom you like best amongst us, and I'll engage to manage the affair entirely to your satisfaction. You may judge in what manner I should have received this compliment in my

own

own country; but I was well enough acquainted with the way of this, to know that he really intended me an obligation, and I thanked him with a very grave curtfey, for his zeal to serve me, and only affured him, I had no occafion to make ufe of it. Thus you fee, my dear, that gallantry and good-breeding are as different, in different climates, as morality and religion. Who have the rightest notions of both, we fhall never know till the day of judgment, for which great day of eclairciffement, I own there is very little impatience in your, &c. &c.

LETTER XI.

To Mrs. J***.

Vienna, Sept. 26, O.S. 1716.

I WAS never more agreeably surprized than by your obliging letter. 'Tis a peculiar mark of my esteem that I tell you so, and I can assure you, that if I loved you one grain less than I do, I should be very sorry to see it so diverting as it is. The mortal aversion I have to writing, makes me tremble at the thoughts of a new correspondent, and I believe I disobliged no less than a dozen of my London acquaintance by refusing to hear from them, though I did verily think they intended to send me very entertaining letters. But I had rather loose the pleasure of reading several witty things, than be forced to write many stupid ones. Yet in spite of these considerations, I am charmed with the proof of your friendship, and beg a continuation of the same goodness,

goodness, though I fear the dulness of this will make you immediately repent of it. It is not from Austria that one can write with vivacity, and I am already infected with the phlegm of the country. Even their amours and their quarrels are carried on with a surprizing temper, and they are never lively, but upon points of ceremony. There, I own, they shew all their passions, and 'tis not long since two coaches meeting in a narrow street at night, the ladies in them not being able to adjust the ceremonial of which should go back, sat there with equal gallantry till two in the morning, and were both so fully determined to die upon the spot rather than yield, in a point of that importance, that the street would never have been cleared till their deaths, if the Emperor had not sent his guards to part them, and even then they refused to stir, till the expedient could be found out, of taking them both out in chairs, exactly in the same moment. After the ladies were agreed, it was with some diffi-culty,

culty, that the pafs was decided between the two coachmen, no lefs tenacious of their rank than the ladies. This paffion is so omnipotent in the breafts of the women, that even their hufbands never die, but they are ready to break their hearts, becaufe that fatal hour puts an end to their rank, no widows having any place at Vienna. The men are not much lefs touched with this point of honour, and they don't only fcorn to marry, but even to make love to any woman of a family not as illuftrious as their own, and the pedigree is much more confidered by them, than either the complexion or features of their miftreffes. Happy are the She's that can number amongft their anceftors, Counts of the Empire; they have neither occafion for beauty, money, nor good conduct to get them hufbands. 'Tis true as to money, 'tis feldom any advantage to the man they marry; the laws of Auftria confine the woman's portion to two thoufand florins (about two hundred pounds Englifh) and whatever

they

they have beside, remains in their own possession and disposal. Thus here are many ladies much richer than their husbands, who are however obliged to allow them pin money agreeable to their quality; and I attribute to this considerable branch of prerogative, the liberty that they take upon other occasions. I am sure you, that know my laziness and extreme indifference on this subject, will pity me, intangled amongst all these ceremonies, which are a wonderful burden to me, though I am the envy of the whole town, having by their own customs the pass before them all. They, indeed, so revenge upon the poor Envoys, this great respect shewed to Ambassadors, that (with all my indifference) I should be very uneasy to suffer it. Upon days of ceremony they have no entrance at court, and on other days must content themselves with walking after every soul, and being the very last taken notice of. But I must write a volume to let you know all the ceremonies, and I have already said too much on so dull a subject, which however employs the whole care of the people here. I need not after this, tell you how agreeably time slides away with me, you know as well as I do the taste of,

Yours, &c. &c.

LETTER XII.

To the Lady X ———.

Vienna, Oct. 1, O. S. 1716.

YOU desire me, Madam, to send you some accounts of the customs here, and at the same time a description of Vienna. I am always willing to obey your commands, but you must upon this occasion take the will for the deed. If I should undertake to tell you all the particulars in which the manners here differ from ours, I must write a whole quire of the dullest stuff that ever was read, or printed without being read. Their dress agrees with the French or English in no one article, but wearing petticoats. They have many fashions peculiar to themselves; they think it indecent for a widow ever to wear green or rose colour, but all the other gayest colours at her own discretion. The assemblies here are the only regular diversion, the operas being always at court,

court, and commonly on some particular occasion. Madam Rabutin, has the assembly constantly every night at her house, and the other ladies, whenever they have a mind to display the magnificence of their apartments, or oblige a friend by complimenting them on the day of their saint, they declare, that on such a day the assembly shall be at their house in honour of the feast of the Count or Countess—such a one. These days are called days of Gala, and all the friends or relations of the lady, whose Saint it is, are obliged to appear in their best cloaths and all their jewels. The mistress of the house takes no particular notice of any body, nor returns any body's visit; and, whoever pleases, may go, without the formality of being presented. The company are entertained with ice in several forms, winter and summer; afterwards they divide into several parties of ombre, piquett, or conversation, all games of hazard being forbid.

I saw

I saw t'other day the Gala for Count Altheim, the Emperor's favourite, and never in my life saw so many fine cloaths ill fancied. They embroider the richest gold stuffs, and provided they can make their cloaths expensive enough, that is all the taste they shew in them. On other days the general dress is a scarf, and what you please under it.

But now I am speaking of Vienna, I am sure you expect I should say something of the convents; they are of all sorts and sizes, but I am best pleased with that of St. Lawrence, where the ease and neatness they seem to live with, appears to me much more edifying than those stricter orders, where perpetual pennance and nastiness must breed discontent and wretchedness. The nuns are all of quality. I think there are to the number of fifty. They have each of them, a little cell perfectly clean, the walls of which are covered with pictures, more or less fine, according to their quality. A long white stone gallery runs by all of them, furnished with the pictures of exemplary sisters; the chapel is extremely neat and richly adorned. But I could not forbear laughing at their shewing me a wooden head of our Saviour, which, they assured me, spoke, during the siege of Vienna; and, as a proof of it, bid me mark his mouth, which had been open ever since. Nothing can be more becoming than the dress of these nuns. It is a white robe, the sleeves of which are turned up with fine white callico, and their head-dress the same, excepting a small veil of black crape that falls behind. They have a lower sort of serving nuns, that wait on them as their chamber-maids. They receive all visits of women, and play at ombre in their chambers with permission of their Abbess, which is very easy to be obtained. I never saw an old woman so good-natured; she is near fourscore, and yet shews very little sign of decay, being still lively and chearful. She caressed me as if I had been her daughter, giving me some pretty things of her own work, and

sweetmeats

sweetmeats in abundance. The grate is not of the most rigid; it is not very hard to put a head through; and I don't doubt but a man, a little more slender than ordinary, might squeeze in his whole person. The young Count of Salamis, came to the grate, while I was there, and the Abbess gave him her hand to kiss. But I was surprized to find here, the only beautiful young woman I have seen at Vienna, and, not only beautiful but genteel, witty and agreeable, of a great family, and who had been the admiration of the town. I could not forbear shewing my surprize at seeing a nun like her. She made me a thousand obliging compliments, and desired me to come often. It would be an infinite pleasure to me, (said she, sighing) but I avoid, with the greatest care, seeing any of my former acquaintance; and whenever they come to our convent, I lock myself in my cell. I observed tears come into her eyes, which touched me exremely, and I began to talk to her in that strain of tender pity

pity she inspired me with; but she would not own to me that she is not perfectly happy. I have since endeavoured to learn the real cause of her retirement, without being able to get any other account, but that every body was surprized at it, and nobody guessed the reason. I have been several times to see her; but it gives me too much melancholy to see so agreeable a young creature buried alive. I am not surprized that nuns have so often inspired violent passions; the pity one naturally feels for them, when they seem worthy of another destiny, making an easy way for yet more tender sentiments. I never in my life had so little charity for the Roman Catholic religion, as since I see the misery it occasions: so many poor unhappy women! and then the gross superstition of the common people, who are some or other of them, day and night, offering bits of candle to the wooden figures, that are set up almost in every street. The processions I see very often are pageantry, as offensive

and

and apparently contradictory to common sense, as the pagods of China. God knows whether it be the womanly spirit of contradiction that works in me, but there never, before, was such zeal against popery in the heart of,

    Dear Madam, &c. &c.

LETTER XIII.

To Mr. ———.

Vienna, Oct. 10, O. S. 1716.

I DESERVE not all the reproaches you make me. If I have been some time without answering your letter, it is not, that I don't know how many thanks are due to you for it; or that I am stupid enough to prefer any amusements to the pleasure of hearing from you; but after the professions of esteem you have so obligingly made me, I cannot help delaying, as long as I can, shewing you, that you are mistaken. If you are sincere, when you say, you expect to be extremely entertained by my letters, I ought to be mortified at the disappointment that I am sure you will receive, when you hear from me; tho' I have done my best endeavours to find out something worth writing to you. I have seen every thing that was to be seen with a very diligent curiosity.

sity. Here are some fine villas, particularly, the late Prince of Lichenstein's: but the statues are all modern, and the pictures not of the first hands. 'Tis true, the Emperor has some of great value. I was yesterday to see the repository, which they call his Treasure, where they seem to have been more diligent in amasing a great quantity of things, than in the choice of them. I spent above five hours there, and yet there were very few things that stopped me long to consider them. But the number is prodigious, being a very long gallery filled, on both sides, and five large rooms. There is a vast quantity of paintings, amongst which are many fine miniatures, but the most valuable pictures are a few of Corregio, those of Titian being at the Favorita.

The cabinet of jewels did not appear to me so rich as I expected to see it. They shewed me here a cup, about the size of a tea-dish, of one entire emerald, which they had so particular a respect for, that only the Emperor has

has the liberty of touching it. There is a large cabinet full of curiosities of clock-work, only one of which I thought worth obferving, that was a craw-fifh with all the motions fo natural, that it was hard to diftinguifh it from the life.

The next cabinet was a large collection of Agates, fome of them extremely beautiful and of an uncommon fize, and feveral vafes of Lapis Lazuli. I was furprized to fee the cabinet of medals fo poorly furnifhed, I did not remark one of any value, and they are kept in a moft ridiculous diforder. As to the Antiques, very few of them deferve that name. Upon my faying they were modern, I could not forbear laughing at the anfwer of the profound antiquary that fhewed them, that " they were ancient enough, for to his knowledge they had been there thefe forty years;" but the next cabinet diverted me yet better, being nothing elfe but a parcel of wax babies, and toys in ivory, very well worthy to be prefented to children of five years

years old. Two of the rooms were wholly filled with these trifles of all kinds, set in jewels, amongst which I was desired to observe a crucifix, that they assured me had spoke very wisely to the Emperor Leopold. I won't trouble you with a catalogue of the rest of the lumber, but I must not forget to mention, a small piece of loadstone that held up an anchor of steel too heavy for me to lift. This is what I thought tye most curious in the whole treasure. There are some few heads of ancient statues; but several of them are defaced by modern additions. I foresee that you will be very little satisfied with this letter, and I dare hardly ask you, to be good-natured enough to charge the dulness of it, on the barrenness of the subject, and to overlook the stupidity of

Your, &c. &c.

LETTER XIV.

To the Countess of ————

Prague, Nov. 17, O.S. 1716.

I HOPE my dear sister wants no new proofs of my sincere affection for her; but I am sure if you do, I could not give you a stronger than writing at this time, after three days, or more properly speaking, three nights and days, hard post travelling.—The kingdom of Bohemia is the most desert of any I have seen in Germany. The villages are so poor, and the post-houses so miserable, that clean straw and fair water are blessings not always to be met with, and better accommodation not to be hoped for. Though I carried my own bed with me, I could not sometimes find a place to set it up in; and I rather chose to travel all night, as cold as it is, wraped up in my furs, than go into the common stoves, which are filled with a mixture of all sorts of ill scents.

This

This town was once the royal seat of the Bohemian Kings, and is still the capital of the kingdom. There are yet some remains of its former splendour, being one of the largest towns in Germany, but, for the most part, old built and thinly inhabited, which makes the houses very cheap. Those people of quality who cannot easily bear the expence of Vienna, chuse to reside here, where they have assemblies, music, and all other diversions, (those of a court excepted) at very moderate rates, all things being here in great abundance, especially, the best wild fowl I ever tasted. I have already been visited by some of the most considerable ladies, whose relations I know at Vienna. They are dressed after the fashions there, after the manner that the people at Exeter imitate those of London; that is, their imitation is more excessive than the original. 'Tis not easy to describe what extraordinary figures they make. The person is so much lost between head-dress and petticoat, that they have as much occasion to write upon their backs, "This is a woman," for the information of travellers, as every sign-post painter had to write, " This is a Bear." I will not forget to write to you again from Dresden and Leipzig, being much more solicitous to content your curiosity, than to indulge my own repose.

I am, &c.

LETTER XV.

To the Countess of ———.

Leipzig, Nov. 21, O.S. 1716.

I BELIEVE, dear sister, you will easily forgive my not writing to you from Dresden, as I promised, when I tell you, that I never went out of my chaise from Prague to this place. You may imagine how heartily I was tired with twenty-four hours post-travelling, without sleep or refreshment (for I can never sleep in a coach however fatigued.) We passed by moon-shine, the frightful precipices that divide Bohemia from Saxony, at the bottom of which runs the river Elbe; but I cannot say, that I had reason to fear drowning in it, being perfectly convinced, that in case of a tumble, it was utterly impossible to come alive to the bottom. In many places the road is so narrow, that I could not discern an inch of space between the wheels and the precipice. Yet I was so good a wife not to wake Mr. W———y, who was fast asleep by my side, to make him share in my fears, since the danger was unavoidable, till I perceived by the bright light of the moon, our postillions nodding on horseback, while the horses were on a full gallop. Then indeed I thought it very convenient to call out to desire them to look where they were going. My calling waked Mr W———y, and he was much more surprised than myself at the situation we were in, and assured me that he passed the Alps five times in different places, without ever having gone a road so dangerous. I have been told since, that 'tis common to find the bodies of travellers in the Elbe, but thank God that was not our destiny, and we came safe to Dresden, so much tired with fear and fatigue, it was not possible for me to compose myself to write. After passing these dreadful rocks, Dresden appeared to me a wonderfully agreeable situation, in a fine large plain on the banks of the Elbe. I was very glad to stay there a day to rest myself. The town is the neatest I have

have seen in Germany; most of the houses are new built; the Elector's palace is very handsome, and his repository full of curiosities of different kinds, with a collection of medals very much esteemed. Sir ———, our King's Envoy, came to see me here, and Madam de L———, whom I knew in London, when her husband was minister to the King of Poland there. She offered me all things in her power to entertain me, and brought some ladies with her, whom she presented to me. The Saxon ladies resemble the Austrian no more, than the Chinese do those of London; they are very genteely dressed after the English and French modes, and have, generally, pretty faces, but they are the most determined *Minaudieres* in the whole world. They would think it a mortal sin against good breeding, if they either spoke or moved in a natural manner. They all affect a little soft lisp, and a pretty pitty-pat step; which female frailties ought, however, to be forgiven them in favour of their civility and good nature to strangers, which I have a great deal of reason to praise.

The Countess of Cozelle is kept prisoner in a melancholy castle, some leagues from hence, and I cannot forbear telling you what I heard of her; because it seems to me very extraordinary, though I foresee I shall swell my letter to the size of a pacquet.—She was mistress to the King of Poland (Elector of Saxony) with so absolute a dominion over him, that never any lady had so much power in that court. They tell a pleasant story of his Majesty's first declaration of love, which he made in a visit to her, bringing in one hand a bag of a hundred thousand crowns, and in the other a horse-shoe, which he snapped asunder before her face, leaving her to draw the consequences of such remarkable proofs of strength and liberality. I know not which charmed her most, but she consented to leave her husband, and to give herself up to him entirely, being divorced publicly, in such a manner, as by their laws permit permits either party to marry again. God knows whether it was at this time, or in some other fond fit, but 'tis certain the King had the weakness to make her a formal contract of marriage; which, though it could signify nothing during the life of the Queen, pleased her so well, that she could not be contented, without telling it to all the people she saw, and giving herself the airs of a Queen. Men endure every thing while they are in love; but when the excess of passion was cooled by long possession, his Majesty begun to reflect on the ill consequences of leaving such a paper in her hands, and desired to have it restored to him. But she rather chose to endure all the most violent effects of his anger than give it up; and though she is one of the richest and most avaricious ladies of her country, she has refused the offer of the continuation of a large pension, and the security of a vast sum of money she has amassed, and has, at last, provoked the King to confine her person to a castle, where she endures all the terrers of a strait imprisonment, and remains still inflexible either to threats or promises. Her violent passions have brought her indeed into fits, which it is supposed will soon put an end to her life. I cannot forbear having some compassion for a woman, that suffers for a point of honour, however mistaken, especially in a country where points of honour are not over scrupulously observed among ladies.

I could have wished Mr. W——'s business had permitted him a longer stay at Dresden.

Perhaps I am partial to a town where they profess the protestant religion, but every thing seemed to me with quite another air of politeness, than I have found in other places. Leipsig, where I am at present, is a town very considerable for its trade, and I take this opportunity of buying page's liveries, gold stuffs for myself, &c. all things of that kind being at least double the price at Vienna, partly because of of the exceffive cuftoms, and partly through want of genius tnd induftry in the people, who make no one fort of thing there, fo that the ladies are obliged to fend even for their fhoes out of Saxony. The fair here is one of the moft confiderable in Germany, and the refort of all the people of quality, as well as of the merchants. This is alfo a fortified town, but I avoid ever mentioning fortifications, being fenfible that I know not how to fpeak of them. I am the more eafy under my ignorance, when I reflect that I am fure you'll willingly forgive the omiffion; for if I made you the moft exact defcription of all the ravelins and baftions I fee in my travels, I dare fwear you would afk me what is a ravelin? and what is a baftion?

Adieu, my dear Sifter.

LETTER XVI.

To the Countess of ————

Brunswick, Nov. 3 O.S. 1716.

I AM just come to Brunswick, a very old town, but which has the advantage of being the capital of the Duke of Wolfenbuttle's dominions, a family (not to speak of its ancient honours) illustrious, by having its younger branch on the throne of England, and having given two Empresses to Germany. I have not forgot to drink your health here in Mum, which I think very well deserves its reputation of being the best in the world. This letter is the third I have wrote to you during my journey, and I declare to you, that if you don't send me immediately a full and true account of all the changes and chances amongst our London acquaintance, I will not write you any description of Hanover, (where I hope to be to-night) though I know you have more curiosity to hear of that place than any other.

LETTER XVII.

To the Countess of B————.

Hanover, Nov. 25, O.S. 1716,

I RECEIVED your ladyship's letter but the day before I left Vienna, though, by the date, I ought to have had it much sooner; but nothing was ever worse regulated than the post in most parts of Germany. I can assure you, the packet at Prague was behind my chaise, and in that manner conveyed to Dresden, so that the secrets of half the country were at my mercy, if I had had any curiosity for them. I would not longer delay my thanks for yours, though the number of my acquaintances here, and my duty of attending at court, leaves me hardly any time to dispose of. I am extremely pleased that I can tell you, without flattery or partiality, that our young Prince* has all the accomplishments that 'tis possible to have at his age, with an air of sprightliness

* The Father of his present Majesty.

and underſtanding, and ſomething ſo very engaging and eaſy in his behaviour, that he needs not the advantage of his rank to appear charming. I had the honour of a long converſation with him laſt night before the King came in. His governor retired on purpoſe (as he told me afterwards) that I might make ſome judgment of his genius, by hearing him ſpeak without conſtraint; and I was ſurprized at the quickneſs and politeneſs, that appeared in every thing he ſaid, joined to a perſon perfectly agreeable, and the fine fair hair of the Princeſs.

This town is neither large nor handſome; but the palace is capable of holding a much greater court than that of St. James's. The King has had the goodneſs to appoint us a lodging in one part of it, without which we ſhould have been very ill accommodated; for the vaſt number of Engliſh crouds the town ſo much, 'tis very good luck to get one ſorry room in a miſerable tavern. I dined to day with the Portugueſe Ambaſſador, who thinks

himſelf

himself very happy to have two wretched parlours in an inn. I have now made the Tour of Germany, and cannot help obferving a confiderable difference between travelling here and in England. One fees none of thofe fine feats of noblemen, fo common amongft us, nor any thing like a country gentleman's houfe, though they have many fituations perfectly fine. But the whole people are divided into abfolute fovereignties, where all the riches and magnificence are at court, or into communities of merchants, fuch as Nurenburg and Frankfort, where they live always in town for the convenience of trade. The King's company of French comedians play here every night. They are very well dreffed, and fome of them not ill actors. His Majefty dines and fups conftantly in public. The court is very numerous, and his affability and goodnefs makes it one of the moft agreeable places in the world.

Dear Madam,

Your L. &c. &c.

LETTER XVIII.

To the Lady R⸺.

Hanover, Oct. 1, O. S. 1716.

I AM very glad, my dear Lady R⸺⸺, that you have been so well pleased, as you tell me, at the report of my returning to England; though, like other pleasures, I can assure you it has no real foundation. I hope you know me enough to take my word against any report concerning me. 'Tis true, as to distance of place, I am much nearer to London than I was some weeks ago; but as to the thoughts of a return, I never was farther off in my life. I own, I could with great joy indulge the pleasing hopes of seeing you and the very few others that share my esteem; but while Mr. W⸺ is determined to proceed in his design, I am determined to follow him.—I am running on upon my own affairs, that is to say, I am going to write very dully, as most people do,

when

when they write of themselves. I will make haste to change the disagreeable subject, by telling you, that I am now got into the region of beauty. All the women have, literally, rosy cheeks, snowy foreheads and bosoms, jet eye-brows, and scarlet lips, to which they generally add coal-black hair. Those perfections never leave them, till the hour of their deaths, and have a very fine effect by candle-light; but I could wish they were handsome with a little more variety. They resemble one another as much as Mrs. Salmon's court of Great-Britain, and are in as much danger of melting away, by too near approaching the fire, which they, for that reason, carefully avoid, though 'tis now such excessive cold weather, that I believe they suffer extremely by that piece of self-denial. The snow is already very deep, and the people begin to slide about in their *Traineaux*. This is a favourite diversion all over Germany. They are little machines fixed upon a sledge, that hold a lady and a gentleman,

and

and are drawn by one horse. The gentleman has the honour of driving, and they move with a prodigious swiftness. The lady, the horse and the *Traineau*, are all as fine as they can be made, and when there are many of them together, 'tis a very agreeable show. At Vienna, where all pieces of magnificence are carried to excess, there are sometimes machines of this kind, that cost five or six hundred pounds English. The Duke of Wolfenbuttle is now at this court; you know he is nearly related to our King, and uncle to the reigning Empress, who is, I believe, the most beautiful princess upon earth. She is now with child, which is all the consolation of the Imperial Court for the loss of the Archduke. I took my leave of her the day before I left Vienna, and she begun to speak to me, with so much grief and tenderness of the death of that young prince, I had much ado to withhold my tears. You know that I am not at all partial to people for their titles; but I own, that I love that charming Princess (if I may use so familiar an expression) and if I had not,

I should

I should have been very much moved at the tragical end of an only son, born, after being so long desired, and at length killed by want of good management, weaning him in the beginning of the winter. Adieu, dear Lady R——, continue to write to me, and believe none of your goodness is lost upon

Yours, &c.

LETTER XIX.

To the Countess of ———

Blankenburg, Oct. 17, O.S. 1716.

I RECEIVED yours, dear sister, the very day I left Hanover. You may easily imagine I was then in too great a hurry to answer it; but you see I take the first opportunity of doing myself that pleasure. I came here the 15th, very late at night, after a terrible journey, in the worst roads and weather that ever poor traveller suffered. I have taken this little fatigue, merely to oblige the reigning Empress, and carry a message from her Imperial Majesty to the Duchess of Blankenburg, her mother, who is a Princess of great address and good breeding, and may be still called a fine woman. It was so late when I came to this town, I did not think it proper to disturb the Duke and Duchess with the news of my arrival;

arrival; so I took up my quarters in a miserable inn; but as soon as I had sent my compliments to their Highnesses, they immediately sent me their own coach and six horses, which had however enough to do to draw us up the very high hill on which the castle is situated. The Duchess is extremely obliging to me, and this little court is not without its diversions. The Duke *taillys* at Basset every night, and the Duchess tells me, she is so well pleased with my company, that it makes her play less than she used to do. I should find it very difficult to steal time to write, if she was not now at church, where I cannot wait on her, not understanding the language enough to pay my devotions in it. You will not forgive me, if I do not say something of Hanover; I cannot tell you that the town is either large or magnificent. The opera-house, which was built by the late elector, is much finer than that of Vienna. I was very sorry that the ill weather did not permit me to see Hernhausen in all its beauty; but in spite of the snow, I thought the gardens very fine. I was particularly surprized at the vast number of orange trees, much larger than any I have ever seen in England, though this climate is certainly colder. But I had more reason to wonder, that night at the King's table, to see a present from a gentleman of this country, of two large baskets full of ripe oranges and lemons of different sorts, many of which were quite new to me; and what I thought worth all the rest, two ripe Ananasses, which, to my taste, are a fruit perfectly delicious. You know they are naturally the growth of Brazil, and I could not imagine how they came here but by enchantment. Upon enquiry, I learnt that they have brought their stoves to such perfection, they lengthen their summer as long as they please, giving to every plant the degree of heat it would receive from the sun in its native soil. The effect is very near the same: I am surprized we do not practice in England so useful an invention. This reflection leads me to consider our obstinacy in shaking with cold

five

five months in the year, rather than make use of stoves, which are certainly one of the greatest conveniences of life. Besides, they are so far from spoiling the form of a room, that they add very much to the magnificence of it, when they are painted and gilt, as they are at Vienna, or at Dresden, where they are often in the shapes of china jars, statues or fine cabinets, so naturally represented, that they are not to be distinguished. If ever I return, in defiance to the fashion, you shall certainly see one in the chamber of,

Dear Sister, Your, &c.

I will write often, since you desire it; but I must beg you to be a little more particular in yours; you fancy me at forty miles distance, and forget, that, after so long an absence, I can't understand hints.

LETTER XX.

To the Lady ———.

Vienna, Jan. 1, O. S. 1717.

I HAVE juſt received here at Vienna, your ladyſhip's compliments on my return to England, ſent me from Hanover. You ſee, madam, all things that are aſſerted with confidence, are not abſolutely true; and that you have no ſort of reaſon to complain of me for making my deſigned return a myſtery to you, when you ſay all the world are informed of it. You may tell all the world in my name, that they are never ſo well informed in my affairs as I am myſelf, that I am very poſitive I am at this time at Vienna, where the carnival is begun, and all ſorts of diverſions are carried to the greateſt height, except that of maſquing, which is never permitted during a war with the Turks. The balls are in public places, where the men pay a gold ducat at entrance, but the ladies nothing. I am told that theſe houſes get ſometimes a thouſand ducats

in

in a night. They are very magnificently furnished, and the music good, if they had not that detestable custom of mixing hunting horns with it, that almost deafen the company. But that noise is so agreeable here, they never make a concert without them. The ball always concludes with English country dances, to the number of thirty or forty couple, and so ill danced, that there is very little pleasure in them. They know but half a dozen, and they have danced them over and over these fifty years. I would fain have taught them some new ones, but I found it would be some months labour to make them comprehend them. Last night there was an Italian comedy acted at court. The scenes were pretty, but the comedy itself such intolerable low farce, without either wit or humour, that I was surprized how all the court could sit there attentively for four hours together. No women are suffered to act on the stage, and the men dressed, like them, were such aukward figures, they very much added to the ridicule of the spectacle. What com-

pleated

pleated the diversion was the excessive cold, which was so great I thought I should have died there. It is now the very extremity of the winter here; the Danube is entirely frozen, and the weather not to be supported without stoves and furs; but, however, the air so clear, almost every body is well, and colds not half so common as in England. I am persuaded there cannot be a purer air, nor more wholesome than that of Vienna. The plenty and excellence of all sorts of provisions are greater here than in any place I ever was before, and 'tis not very expensive to keep a splendid table. 'Tis really a pleasure to pass through the markets, and see the abundance of what we should think rarities, of fowls and venison, that are daily brought in from Hungary and Bohemia. They want nothing but shell-fish, and are so fond of oysters, that they have them sent from Venice, and eat them very greedily, stink or not stink. Thus I obey your commands, Madam, in giving you an account of Vienna, though I know you

will

will not be satisfied with it. You chide me for my laziness in not telling you a thousand agreeable and surprizing things, that you say you are sure I have seen and heard. Upon my word, Madam, 'tis my regard to truth, and not laziness, that I do not entertain you with as many prodigies as other travellers use to divert their readers with. I might easily pick up wonders in every town I pass through, or tell you a long series of popish miracles, but I cannot fancy that there is any thing new in letting you know that priests will lie, and the mob believe, all the world over. Then as for news, as you are so inquisitive about, how can it be entertaining to you (that don't know the people) that the Prince of —— has forsaken the Countess of ——? or that the Prince such-a-one, has an intrigue with Count such-a-one? Would you have me write novels, like the Countess of D'——? and is it not better to tell you a plain truth,

That I am, &c.

LETTER XXI.

To the Countess of ————

Vienna, Jan. 16, O. S. 1717.

I AM now, dear sister, to take leave of you for a long time, and of Vienna for ever, designing, to-morrow, to begin my journey through Hungary in spite of the excessive cold, and deep snows, which is enough to damp a greater courage than I am mistress of. But my principle of passive obedience, carries me through every thing. I have had my audience of leave of the Empress. His Imperial Majesty was pleased to be present when I waited on the reigning Empress, and after a very obliging conversation, both their Imperial Majesties invited me to take Vienna in my road back; but I have no thoughts of enduring over again, so great a fatigue. I delivered a letter from the Duchess of Blankenburg. I staid but a few days at that court, though her Highness pressed

pressed me very much to stay; and when I left her, engaged me to write to her. I wrote you a long letter from thence, which I hope you have received, though you don't mention it; but I believe I forgot to tell you one curiosity in all the German courts, which I cannot forbear taking notice of: All the Princes keep favourite dwarfs. The Emperor and Empress have two of these little monsters, as ugly as devils, especially the female; but they are all bedaubed with diamonds, and stand at her Majesty's elbow in all public places. The Duke of Wolfenbuttle has one, and the Duchess of Blankenburg is not without hers, but indeed the most proportionable I ever saw. I am told the King of Denmark has so far improved upon this fashion, that his dwarf is his chief minister. I can assign no reason for their fondness for these pieces of deformity, but the opinion all the absolute Princes have, that 'tis below them to converse with the rest of mankind; and not to be quite alone, they are forced to seek their companions among the refuse of human nature,

these

these creatures being the only part of their court privileged to talk freely to them. I am at present confined to my chamber by a sore throat, and am really glad of the excuse to avoid seeing people, that I love well enough to be very much mortified when I think I am going to part with them for ever. 'Tis true the Austrians are not commonly the most polite people in the world, nor the most agreeable. But Vienna is inhabited by all nations, and I had formed to myself a little society of such as were perfectly to my own taste. And though the number was not very great, I could never pick up, in any other place, such a number of reasonable, agreeable people. We were almost always together, and you know I have ever been of opinion, that a chosen conversation, composed of a few that one esteems, is the greatest happiness of life. Here are some Spaniards of both sexes that have all the vivacity and generosity of sentiments anciently ascribed to their nation; and could I believe, that the whole kingdom were like them, I would wish

nothing

nothing more than to end my days there. The ladies of my acquaintance have so much goodness for me, they cry whenever they see me, since I have determined to undertake this journey. And, indeed, I am not very easy when I reflect on what I am going to suffer. Almost every body I see frights me with some new difficulty. Prince Eugene has been so good as to say all things he could to persuade me to stay till the Danube is thawed, that I may have the conveniency of going by water, assuring me, that the houses in Hungary are such, as are no defence against the weather, and that I shall be obliged to travel three or four days between Bude and Esseek, without finding any house at all, through desart plains covered with snow; where the cold is so violent, many have been killed by it. I own these terrors have made a very deep impression on my mind, because I believe he tells me things truly as they are, and no body can be better informed of them. Now I have named that great man, I am sure you expect, I should say something

particular

particular of him, having the advantage of seeing him very often; but I am as unwilling to speak of him at Vienna, as I should be to talk of Hercules in the court of Omphale, if I had seen him there. I don't know what comfort other people find in considering the weakness of great men, (because, perhaps, it brings them nearer to their level) but 'tis always a mortification to me, to observe that there is no perfection in humanity. The young Prince of Portugal is the admiration of the whole court; he is handsome and polite with a great vivacity. All the officers tell wonders of his gallantry the last campaign. He is lodged at court with all the honours due to his rank.— Adieu, dear sister; this is the last account you will have from me of Vienna. If I survive my journey, you shall hear from me again. I can say, with great truth, in the words of Monefes, "I have long learnt to hold myself as nothing;" but when I think of the fatigue my poor infant must suffer, I have all a mother's fondness in my eyes, and all her tender passion in my heart.

P. S.

P. S. I have written a letter to my lady ———, that I believe she won't like; and upon cooler reflection, I think I had done better to have let it alone; but I was downright peevish at all her queſtions, and her ridiculous imagination, that I have certainly ſeen abundance of wonders which I keep to myſelf out of meer malice. She is very angry that I won't lye like other travellers. I verily believe ſhe expects I ſhould tell her of the Anthropophagic, men whoſe heads grow below their ſhoulders; however, pray ſay ſomething to pacify her.

LETTER XXII.
To Mr. Pope.
Vienna, Jan. 16, O.S. 1717.

I HAVE not time to answer your letter, being in the hurry of preparing for my journey; but, I think, I ought to bid adieu to my friends with the same solemnity, as if I was going to mount a breach, at least, if I am to believe the information of the people here, who denounce all sorts of terrors to me; and, indeed, the weather is at present such as very few ever set out in. I am threatened, at the same time, with being frozen to death, buried in the snow, and taken by the Tartars, who ravage that part of Hungary I am to pass. 'Tis true, we shall have a considerable escorte, so that, possibly, I may be diverted with a new scene, by finding myself in the midst of a battle. How my adventures will conclude, I leave entirely to providence; if comically, you shall hear of them.—Pray be so good as to tell Mr. —— I have received his letter. Make him my adieus; if I live, I will answer it. The same compliment to my Lady R——.

LETTER XXIII.

To the Countefs of ———

Peterwaradin, Jan. 30, O.S. 1717.

AT length, dear fifter, I am fafely arrived with all my family in good health at Peterwaradin; having fuffered fo little from the rigour of the feafon (againft which we were all provided by furs) and found fuch tolerable accommodation every where, by the care of fending before, that I can hardly forbear laughing when I recollect all the frightful ideas that were given me of this journey. Thefe, I fee, were wholly owing to the tendernefs of my Vienna friends, and their defire of keeping me with them for this winter. Perhaps it will not be difagreeable to you to give a fhort journal of my journey, being through a country entirely unknown to you, and very little paffed, even by the Hungarians themfelves, who generally chufe to take the conveniency of going down the Danube. We have had the bleffing of being favoured with finer weather than is common at this time of the year; though the snow was so deep, we were obliged to have our own coaches fixed upon *Traineaus*, which move so swift and so easily, 'tis by far the most agreeable manner of travelling post. We came to Raab (the second day from Vienna) on the seventeenth instant, where Mr. W— sending word of our arrival to the governor, the best house in the town was provided for us, the garrison put under arms, a guard ordered at our door, and all other honours paid to us. The governor and all other officers immediately waited on Mr. W——, to know if there was any thing to be done for his service. The bishop of Temeswar came to visit us, with great civility, earnestly pressing us to dine with him next day, which we refusing, as being resolved to pursue our journey, he sent us several baskets of winter fruit, and a great variety of Hungarian wines, with a young hind just killed. This is a prelate of great power in this country, of the ancient family of Nadasti, so considerable,

considerable, for many ages, in this kingdom. He is a very polite, agreeable, chearful old man, wearing the Hungarian habit, with a venerable white beard down to his girdle.—Raab is a strong town, well garrisoned and fortified, and was a long time the frontier town between the Turkish and German Empires. It has its name from the river Rab, on which it is situated, just on its meeting with the Danube, in an open champain country. It was first taken by the Turks under the command of Bassa Sinan, in the reign of Sultan Amurath III. in the year fifteen hundred ninety four. The governor being supposed to have betrayed it, was afterwards beheaded by the Emperor's command. The Counts of Swartzenburg and Palfi retook it by surprize 1598, since which time it has remained in the hands of the Germans, though the Turks once more attempted to gain it by stratagem in 1642. The cathedral is large and well built, which is all I saw remarkable in the town. Leaving Comora on the other side the river, we went the eighteenth to Nofmuhl, a fmall village, where, however, we made fhift to find tolerable accommodation. We continued two days travelling between this place and Buda, through the fineſt plains in the world, as even as if they were paved, and extremely fruitful; but for the moſt part defart and uncultivated, laid waſte by the long wars between the Turk and the Emperor; and the more cruel civil war, occaſioned by the barbarous perſecution of the Proteſtant religion, by the Emperor Leopold. That Prince has left behind him the character of an extraordinary piety, and was naturally of a mild merciful temper; but, putting his conſcience into the hands of a jeſuit, he was more cruel and-treacherous to his poor Hungarian ſubjects, than ever the Turk has been to the Chriſtians; breaking, without ſcruple, his coronation oath, and his faith ſolemnly given in many public treaties. Indeed nothing can be more melancholy than in travelling through Hungary, to reflect on the former flouriſhing ſtate of that kingdom, and to ſee ſuch a noble ſpot

of

of earth almoſt uninhabited. Such are alſo the preſent circumſtances of Buda, (where we arrived very early the twenty-ſecond) once the royal ſeat of the Hungarian kings, whoſe palace there, was reckoned one of the moſt beautiful buildings of the age, now wholly deſtroyed, no part of the town having been repaired ſince the laſt ſiege, but the fortifications and the caſtle, which is the preſent reſidence of the governor general Ragule, an officer of great merit. He came immediately to ſee us, and carried us in his coach to his houſe, where I was received by his lady, with all poſſible civility, and magnificently entertained. This city is ſituated upon a little hill on the ſouth ſide of the Danube. The caſtle is much higher than the town, and from it the proſpect is very noble. Without the walls lie a vaſt number of little houſes or rather huts, that they call the Raſcian town, being altogether inhabited by that people. The governor aſſured me it would furniſh twelve thouſand fighting men. Theſe towns look very odd; their houſes ſtand in rows many thousand of them so close together, that they appear, at a little distance, like old-fashioned thatched tents. They consist, every one of them, of one hovel above, and another under ground; these are their summer and winter apartments. Buda was first taken by Solyman the Magnificent, in 1526, and lost the following year to Ferdinand the First, King of Bohemia. Solyman regained it by the treachery of the garrison, and voluntarily gave it into the hands of King John of Hungary, after whose death, his son being an infant, Ferdinand laid siege to it, and the Queen mother was forced to call Solyman to her aid. He indeed raised the siege; but left a Turkish garrison in the town, and commanded her to remove her court from thence, which she was forced to submit to in 1541. It resisted afterwards the sieges laid to it, by the Marquis of Brandenburg, in the year 1542; Count Schwartzenburgh, 1598; General Rosworm, in 1602; and the Duke of Lorrain, commander of the Emperor's forces, in 1684, to whom it yielded in 1686, after an obstinate

obstinate defence, Apti Bassa, the governor, being killed, fighting in the breach, with a Roman bravery. The loss of this town was so important, and so much resented by the Turks, that it occasioned the deposing of their Emperor Mahomet the Fourth, the year following.

We did not proceed on our journey till the twenty-third, when we passed through Adam and Todowar, both considerable towns, when in the hands of the Turks, but now quite ruined. The remains, however, of some Turkish towns, shew something of what they have been. This part of the country is very much over-grown with wood, and little frequented. 'Tis incredible what vast numbers of wild fowl we saw, which often live here to a good old age,——and " undisturb'd by guns, in quiet sleep."—We came the five and twentieth to Mohatch, and were shewed the field near it, where Lewis, the young King of Hungary, lost his army and his life, being drowned in a

ditch

ditch, trying to fly from Balybeus, general of Solyman the Magnificent. This battle opened the firſt paſſage for the Turks into the heart of Hungary.——I don't name to you the little villages, of which I can ſay nothing remarkable; but I'll aſſure you, I have always found a warm ſtove and great plenty, particularly of wildboar, veniſon, and all kinds of Gibier. The few people that inhabit Hungary, live eaſily enough; they have no money; but the woods and plains afford them proviſion in great abundance: they were ordered to give us all things neceſſary, even what horſes we pleaſed to demand, gratis; but Mr. W—— would not oppreſs the poor country people, by making uſe of this order, and always paid them to the full worth of what we had. They were ſo ſurpriſed at this unexpected generoſity, which they are very little uſed to, that they always preſſed upon us, at parting, a dozen of fat pheaſants, or ſomething of that ſort for a preſent. Their dreſs is very primitive, being only a plain ſheep's ſkin, and a cap and boots

of

of the some stuff. You may easily imagine this lasts them many winters; and thus they have very little occasion for money. The twenty-sixth, we passed over the frozen Danube, with all our equipage, and carriages. We met, on the other side, general Veterani, who invited us, with great civility, to pass the night at a little castle of his, a few miles off, assuring us we should have a very hard day's journey to reach Essek. This we found but too true, the woods being very dangerous, and scarce passable, from the vast quantity of wolves that hoard in them. We came however, safe, though late, to Essek, where we stayed a day, to dispatch a courier with letters to the Bassa of Belgrade; and I took that opportunity of seeing the town, which is not very large, but fair built and well fortified. This was a town of great trade, very rich and populous, when in the hands of the Turks. It is situated on the Drave, which runs into the Danube. The bridge was esteemed one of the most extraordinary in the world, being eight thousand paces long, and all built of oak. It

was

was burnt, and the city laid in ashes by Count Lefly, 1685, but was again repaired and fortified by the Turks, who however abandoned it in 1687. General Dunnewalt then took possession of it for the Emperor, in whose hands it has remained ever since, and is esteemed one of the bulwarks of Hungary. The twenty-eighth we went to Bocorwar, a very large Rascian town, all built after the manner I have described to you. We were met there by Colonel ——, who would not suffer us to go any where but to his quarters, where I found his wife, a very agreeable Hungarian lady, and his niece and daughter, two pretty young women, crowded into three or four Rascian houses, cast into one, and made as neat and convenient as those places are capable of being made. The Hungarian ladies are much handsomer than those of Austria. All the Vienna beauties are of that country. They are generally very fair and well shaped, and their dress, I think, is extremely becoming. This lady was in a gown of scarlet velvet, lined and faced with sables, made exact to her shape, and the skirt falling

to

to her feet. The sleeves are strait to their arms, and the stays buttoned before, with two rows of little buttons of gold, pearl, or diamonds. On their heads they wear a tassel of gold, that hangs low on one side, lined with sable, or some other fine fur.——They gave us a handsome dinner, and I thought the conversation very polite and agreeable. They would accompany us part of our way.—The twenty-ninth, we arrived here, where we were met by the commanding officer at the head of all the officers of the garrison. We are lodged in the best apartment of the governor's house, and entertained in a very splendid manner, by the Emperor's order. We wait here till all points are adjusted, concerning our reception on the Turkish frontiers. Mr. W———'s courier, which he sent from Esek, returned this morning, with the Bassa's answer in a purse of scarlet sattin, which the Interpreter here has translated. 'Tis to promise him to be honourably received. I desired him to appoint where he would be met, by the Turkish convoy.——He has dispatched the courier back, naming

naming Betſko, a village in the midway between Peterwaradin and Belgrade. We ſhall ſtay here till we receive his anſwer.——Thus, dear ſiſter, I have given you a very particular, and (I am afraid you'll think) a tedious account of this part of my travels. It was not an affectation of ſhewing my reading that has made me tell you ſome little ſcraps of the hiſtory of the towns I have paſſed through. I have always avoided any thing of that kind, when I ſpoke of places that I believe you knew the ſtory of, as well as myſelf. But Hungary being a part of the world, which I believe quite new to you, I thought you might read with ſome pleaſure an account of it, which I have been very ſolicitous to get from the beſt hands. However, if you don't like it, 'tis in your power to forbear reading it. I am,

Dear Siſter,

I am promiſed to have this letter carefully ſent to Vienna.

LETTER XXIV.

To Mr. Pope.

Belgrade, Feb. 12, O. S. 1717.

I DID verily intend to write to you a long letter from Peterwaradin, where I expected to stay three or four days, but the Bassa here was in such haste to see us, that he dispatched the courier back (which Mr. W— had sent to know the time he would send the convoy to meet us) without suffering him to pull off his boots. My letters were not thought important enough to stop our journey, and we left Peterwaradin the next day, being waited on by the chief officers of the garrison, and a considerable convoy of Germans and Rascians. The Emperor has several regiments of these people; but, to say the truth, they are rather plunderers than soldiers; having no pay, and being obliged to furnish their own arms and horses; they rather look like vagabond gypsies, or stout beggars, than regular troops.

I can-

I cannot forbear speaking a word of this race of creatures, who are very numerous all over Hungary. They have a patriarch of their own at Grand Cairo, and are really of the Greek church, but their extreme ignorance gives their priests occasion to impose several new notions upon them. These fellows letting their hair and beard grow inviolate, make exactly the figure of the Indian Bramins. They are heirs general to all the money of the laiety; for which, in return, they give them formal passports signed and sealed for Heaven; and the wives and children only inherit the house and cattle. In most other points they follow the Greek church.—This little digression has interrupted my telling you we passed over the fields of Carlowitz, where the last great victory was obtained by Prince Eugene over the Turks. The marks of that glorious bloody day are yet recent, the field being yet strewed with the skulls and carcasses of unburied men, horses, and camels. I could not look without horror on such numbers of mangled human bodies,

nor

nor without reflecting on the injustice of war, that makes murther not only necessary but meritorious. Nothing seems to be plainer proof of the irrationality of mankind (whatever fine claims we pretend to reason) than the rage with which they contest for a small spot of ground, when such vast parts of fruitful earth lie quite uninhabited. 'Tis true, custom has now made it unavoidable; but can there be a greater demonstration of want of reason, than a custom being firmly established, so plainly contrary to the interest of man in general? I am a good deal inclined to believe Mr. Hobbs, that the state of nature, is a state of war; but thence I conclude human nature not rational, if the word reason means common sense, as I suppose it does. I have a great many admirable arguments to support this reflection; I won't however trouble you with them, but return, in a plain style, to the history of my travels.

We were met at Betsko (a village in the midway between Belgrade and Peterwaradin) by an Aga of the Janizaries, with a body of Turks

Turks, exceeding the Germans by one hundred men, though the Bassa had engaged to send exactly the same number. You may judge by this of their fears. I am really persuaded, that they hardly thought the odds of one hundred men set them even with the Germans; however, I was very uneasy till they were parted, fearing some quarrel might arise notwithstanding the parole given. We came late to Belgrade, the deep snows making the ascent to it very difficult. It seems a strong city, fortified, on the east side, by the Danube; and on the south, by the river Save, and was formerly the barrier of Hungary. It was first taken by Solyman the Magnificent; and since by the Emperor's forces, led by the Elector of Bavaria. The Emperor held it only two years, it being retaken by the Grand Vizier. It is now fortified with the utmost care and skill the Turks are capable of, and strengthened by a very numerous garrison of their bravest Janizaries, commanded by a Bassa Serasskier (i.e. General;) though this last expression is not very just;

for

for to say truth, the Seraskier is commanded by the Janizaries. These troops have an absolute authority here, and their conduct carries much more the aspect of rebellion, than the appearance of subordination. You may judge of this by the following story, which at the same time will give you an idea of the admirable intelligence of the Governor of Peterwaradin, though so few hours distant. We were told by him at Peterwaradin, that the garrison and inhabitants of Belgrade were so weary of the war, they had killed their Bassa about two months ago, in a mutiny, because he had suffered himself to be prevailed upon by a bribe of five purses (five hundred pound sterling) to give permission to the Tartars to ravage the German frontiers. We were very well pleased to hear of such favourable dispositions in the people, but when we came hither, we found the governor had been ill informed, and the real truth of the story to be this. The late Bassa fell under the displeasure of his soldiers, for no other reason, but restraining their incursions on the Germans. They took it into their heads from that mildnefs, that he had intelligence with the enemy, and fent fuch information to the Grand Signior at Adrianople; but redrefs not coming quick enough from thence, they affembled themfelves in a tumultous manner, and by force dragged their Baffa before the Cadi and Mufti, and there demanded juftice in a mutinous way; one crying out, Why he protected the Infidels? Another, Why he fqueezed them of their money? The Baffa, eafily gueffing their purpofe, calmly replied to them, that they afked him too many queftions, and that he had but one life, which muft anfwer for all. They then immediately fell upon him with their fcymitars, (without waiting the fentence of their heads of the law) and in a few moments cut him in pieces. The prefent Baffa has not dared to punifh the murder; on the contrary, he affected to applaud the actors of it, as brave fellows, that knew how to do themfelves juftice. He takes all pretences of throwing money among the garrifon, rison, and suffers them to make little excursions into Hungary, where they burn some poor Rascian houses.

You may imagine, I cannot be very easy in a town which is really under the government of an insolent soldiery.——We expected to be immediately dismissed, after a night's lodging here; but the Bassa detains us till he receives orders from Adrianople, which may, possibly be a month a coming. In the mean time, we are lodged in one of the best houses, belonging to a very considerable man amongst them, and have a whole chamber of Janizaries to guard us. My only diversion is the conversation of our host Achmet-beg, a title something like that of Count in Germany. His father was a great Bassa, and he has been educated in the most polite Eastern learning, being perfectly skilled in the Arabic and Persian languages, and an extraordinary scribe, which they call Effendi. This accomplishment makes way to the greatest preferments; but he has had the good sense to prefer an easy, quiet, secure life, to all the dangerous honours of the Porte. He sups with us every night, and drinks wine very freely. You cannot imagine how much he is delighted with the liberty of conversing with me. He has explained to me several pieces of Arabian poetry, which, I observe, are in numbers, not unlike ours, generally of an alternate verse, and of a very musical sound. Their expressions of love are very passionate and lively. I am so much pleased with them, I really believe I should learn to read Arabic, if I was to stay here a few months. He has very good library of their books of all kinds; and, as he tells me, spends the greatest part of his life there. I pass for a great scholar with him, by relating to him some of the Persian tales, which I find are genuine. At first, he believed I understood Persian. I have frequent disputes with him, concerning the difference of our customs, particularly the confinement of women. He assures me, there is nothing at all in it; only, says he, we have the advantage, that when our

wives

wives cheat us, no body knows it. He has wit, and is more polite than many Christian men of quality. I am very much entertained with him.—He has had the curiosity to make one of our servants set him an alphabet of our letters, and can already write a good Roman hand. But these amusements do not hinder my wishing heartily to be out of this place; though the weather is colder than I believe it ever was, any where, but in Greenland —— We have a very large stove constantly kept hot, and yet the windows of the room are frozen on the inside.———God knows when I may have an opportunity of sending this letter; but I have written it, for the discharge of my own conscience; and you cannot now reproach me, that one of yours makes ten of mine. Adieu.

LETTER XXV.

To her Royal Highness the Princess of Wales.*

Adrianople, April 1, O. S. 1717.

I HAVE now, Madam, finished a journey that has not been undertaken by any Christian, since the time of the Greek Emperors; and I shall not regret all the fatigues I have suffered in it, if it gives me an opportunity of amusing your R. H. by an account of places utterly unknown amongst us; the Emperor's Ambassadors, and those few English that have come hither, always going on the Danube to Nicopolis. But the river was now frozen, and Mr. W— was so zealous for the service of his Majesty, that he would not defer his journey to wait for the conveniency of that passage. We crossed the deserts of Servia, almost quite over-grown with wood, though a country naturally fertile. The inhabitants are industrious; but the oppression of the peasants is so great, they are forced to abandon their

* The late Queen Caroline.

their houses, and neglect their tillage, all they have being a prey to the Janizaries, whenever they please to seize upon it. We had a guard of five hundred of them, and I was almost in tears every day, to see their insolencies in the poor villages through which we passed.—After seven days travelling through thick woods, we came to Nissa, once the capital of Servia, situated in a fine plain on the river Nissava, in a very good air, and so fruitful a soil, that the great plenty is hardly credible. I was certainly assured, that the quantity of wine last vintage was so prodigious, that they were forced to dig holes in the earth to put it in, not having vessels enough in the town to hold it. The happiness of this plenty is scarce perceived by the oppressed people. I saw here a new occasion for my compassion. The wretches that had provided twenty waggons for our baggage from Belgrade hither for a certain hire, being all sent back without payment, some of their horses lamed, and others killed, without any satisfaction made for them. The poor fellows came round the house weeping and tearing their hair

and

and beards in a most pitiful manner, without getting any thing but drubs from the insolent soldiers. I cannot express to your R. H. how much I was moved at this scene. I would have paid them the money, out of my own pocket, with all my heart; but it would have been only giving so much to the Aga, who would have taken it from them without any remorse. After four days journey from this place over the mountains, we came to Sophia, situated in a large beautiful plain on the river Isca, and surrounded with distant mountains. 'Tis hardly possible to see a more agreeable landskip. The city itself is very large and extremely populous. Here are hot baths, very famous for their medicinal virtues.———Four days journey from hence we arrived at Philippopolis, after having passed the ridges between the mountains of Haemus and Rhodope, which are always covered with snow. This town is situated on a rising ground, near the river Hebrus, and is almost wholly inhabited by Greeks; here are still some ancient Christian churches.

They

They have a bishop; and several of the richest Greeks live here; but they are forced to conceal their wealth with great care, the appearance of poverty (which includes part of its inconveniences) being all their security against feeling it in earnest. The country from hence to Adrianople, is the finest in the world. Vines grow wild on all the hills, and the perpetual spring they enjoy, makes every thing gay and flourishing. But this climate, happy as it seems, can never be preferred to England, with all its frosts and snows, while we are blessed with an easy government, under a king, who makes his own happiness consist in the liberty of his people, and chooses rather to be looked upon as their father than their master.—This theme would carry me very far, and I am sensible I have already tired out your R. H's patience. But my letter is in your hands, and you may make it as short as you please, by throwing it into the fire, when weary of reading it. I am, Madam,

With the greatest respect.

LETTER XXVI.

To the Lady ———.

Adrianople. April 1, O. S. 1717.

I AM now got into a new world, where every thing I see appears to me a change of scene; and I write to your ladyship, with some content of mind, hoping, at least, that you will find the charm of novelty in my letters, and no longer reproach me, that I tell you nothing extraordinary. I won't trouble you with a relation of our tedious journey; but I must not omit what I saw remarkable at Sophia, one of the most beautiful towns in the Turkish empire, and famous for its hot baths, that are resorted to both for diversion and health. I stopt here one day, on purpose to see them; and designing to go incognito, I hired a Turkish coach. These *voitures* are not at all like ours, but much more convenient for the country, the heat being so great that glasses would be very troublesome. They are made a good deal in the manner of the Dutch stage coaches, having wooden lattices painted and gilded; the inside being also painted with baskets and nosegays of flowers, intermixed commonly with little poetical mottos. They are covered all over with scarlet cloth, lined with silk, and very often richly embroidered and fringed.— This covering entirely hides the persons in them, but may be thrown back at pleasure, and thus permit the ladies to peep through the lattices. They hold four people very conveniently, seated on cushions, but not raised.

In one of these covered waggons, I went to the Bagnio about ten o'clock. It was already full of women. It is built of stone, in the shape of a dome, with no windows but in the roof, which gives light enough. There were five of these domes joining together, the outmost being less than the rest, and serving only as a hall, where the portress stood at the door. Ladies of quality generally give this woman a crown or ten shillings, and I did not forget that ceremony. The next room is a very large one,

paved

paved with marble, and all round it are two raised Sofas of marble, one above another. There were four fountains of cold water in this room, falling first into marble basons, and then running on the floor in little channels made for that purpose, which carried the streams into the next room, something less than this, with the same sort of marble sofas, but so hot with steams of sulphur, proceeding from the baths joining to it, 'twas impossible to stay there with one's clothes on. The two other domes were the hot baths, one of which had cocks of cold water turning into it, to temper it to what degree of warmth the bathers pleased to have.

I was in my travelling habit, which is a riding dress, and certainly appeared very extraordinary to them. Yet there was not one of them that shewed the least surprize or impertinent curiosity, but received me with all the obliging civility possible. I know no European court, where the ladies would have behaved themselves in so polite a manner to such a stranger. I believe, upon the whole, there were two hundred women,

women, and yet none of those disdainful smiles, and satirical whispers, that never fail in our assemblies, when any body appears that is not dressed exactly in the fashion. They repeated over and over to me: " UZELLE, PEK UZELLE," which is nothing but " charming, very charming."——The first sofas were covered with cushions and rich carpets, on which sat the ladies; and on the second, their slaves behind them, but without any distinction of rank by their dress, all being in the state of nature, that is, in plain English, stark naked, without any beauty or defect concealed. Yet there was not the least wanton smile or immodest gesture among them. They walked and moved with the same majestic grace, which Milton describes our General Mother with. There were many amongst them, as exactly proportioned as ever any goddess was drawn by the pencil of a Guido or Titian,—and most of their skins shiningly white, only adorned by their beautiful hair, divided into many tresses, hanging on their shoulders, braided either with

pearl

pearl or ribbon, perfectly representing the figures of the graces.

I was here convinced of the truth of a reflection I have often made, that if it were the fashion to go naked, the face would be hardly observed. I perceived that the ladies of the most delicate skins and finest shapes, had the greatest share of my admiration, though their faces were sometimes less beautiful than those of their companions. To tell you the truth, I had wickedness enough to wish secretly, that Mr. Gervais could have been there invisible. I fancy it would have very much improved his art, to see so many fine women naked in different postures, some in conversation, some working, others drinking coffee or sherbert, and many negligently lying on their cushions, while their slaves (generally pretty girls of seventeen or eighteen) were employed in braiding their hair in several pretty fancies. In short, 'tis the woman's coffee-house, where all the news of the town is told, scandal invented, &c.—

They

They generally take this diverſion once a week, and ſtay there at leaſt four or five hours, without getting cold by immediate coming out of the hot-bath into the cold room, which was very ſurpriſing to me. The lady that ſeemed the moſt conſiderable among them, entreated me to ſit by her, and would fain have undreſſed me for the bath. I excuſed myſelf with ſome difficulty. They being, however, all ſo earneſt in perſuading me, I was at laſt forced to open my ſhirt, and ſhew them my ſtays, which ſatisfied them very well; for, I ſaw, they believed I was locked up in that machine, and that it was not in my own power to open it, which contrivance they attributed to my huſband.—I was charmed with their civility and beauty, and ſhould have been very glad to paſs more time with them; but Mr. W—— reſolving to purſue his journey next morning early, I was in haſte to ſee the ruins of Juſtinian's church, which did not afford me ſo agreeable a proſpect as I had left, being little more than a heap of ſtones.

Adieu,

Adieu, Madam, I am sure I have now entertained you with an account of such a sight, as you never saw in your life, and what no book of travels could inform you of, as 'tis no less than death for a man to be found in one of these places.

LETTER XXVII.

To the Abbot ——.

Adrianople, April 1, O.S. 1717.

YOU see that I am very exact in keeping the promise you engaged me to make. I know not, however, whether your curiosity will be satisfied with the accounts I shall give you, tho' I can assure you, the desire I have to oblige you to the utmost of my power, has made me very diligent in my enquiries and observations. 'Tis certain we have but very imperfect accounts of the manners and religion of these people. This part of the world being seldom visited, but by merchants, who mind little but their own affairs; or travellers, who make too short a stay to be able to report any thing exactly of their own knowledge. The Turks are too proud to converse familiarly with merchants, who can give no better account of the ways here, than a French Refugee, lodging in a garret in Greek-street, could write of the court of England. The journey we have made from Belgrade hither, cannot possibly be passed by any out of a public character. The desert woods of Servia, are the common refuge of thieves, who rob, fifty in a company, so that we had need of all our guards to secure us; and the villages are so poor, that only force could extort from them necessary provisions. Indeed the Janizaries had no mercy on their poverty, killing all the poultry and sheep they could find, without asking to whom they belonged; while the wretched owners durst not put in their claim for fear of being beaten. Lambs just fallen, geese and turkies big with egg, all massacred without distinction! I fancied I heard the complaints of Melibeus, for the hope of his flock. When the Bassas travel, 'tis yet worse. Those oppressors are not content with eating all that is to be eaten belonging to the peasants; after they have crammed themselves and their numerous retinue, they have the impudence to exact what they call

call Teeth-money, a contribution for their use of their teeth, worn with doing them the honour of devouring their meat. This is literally and exactly true, however extravagant it may seem; and such is the natural corruption of a military government, their religion not allowing of this barbarity, any more than ours does.

I had the advantage of lodging three weeks at Belgrade, with a principal Effendi, that is to say, a scholar. This set of men are equally capable of preferments in the law or the church; those two sciences being cast into one, and a lawyer and a priest being the same word in the Turkish language. They are the only men really considerable in the Empire, all the profitable employments and church revenues are in their hands. The Grand Signior, though general heir to his people, never presumes to touch their lands or money, which go, in an uninterrupted succession, to their children. 'Tis true, they lose this privilege, by accepting a place at court, or the title of Bassa; but there are few examples of such fools among them. You may easily judge of the power of these men, who have engrossed all the learning and almost all the wealth of the Empire. 'Tis they that are the real authors, tho' the soldiers are the actors of revolutions. They deposed the late Sultan Mustapha, and their power is well known, that 'tis the Emperor's interest to flatter them.

This is a long digression. I was going to tell you, that an intimate, daily conversation with the Effendi Achmet-beg, gave me an opportunity of knowing their religion and morals in a more particular manner than perhaps any Christian ever did. I explained to him the difference between the religion of England and Rome; and he was pleased to hear there were Christians, that did not worship images, or adore the Virgin Mary. The ridicule of transubstantiation appeared very strong to him. Upon comparing our creeds together, I am convinced, that if our friend Dr. —— had free liberty of preaching here, it would be very

easy

easy to perswade the generality to Christianity, whose notions are very little different from his. Mr. Whiston would make a very good apostle here. I don't doubt but his zeal will be much fired, if you communicate this account to him; but tell him, he must first have the gift of tongues, before he can possibly be of any use.——Mahometism is divided into as many sects as Christianity, and the first institution as much neglected and obscured by interpretations. I cannot here forbear reflecting on the natural inlination of mankind, to make mysteries and novelties.——The Zeidi, Kudi, Jabari, &c. put me in mind of the Catholics, Lutherans, and Calvinists, and are equally zealous against one another. But the most prevailing opinion, if you search into the secret of the Effendi's, is plain Deism. This is indeed kept from the people, who are amused with a thousand different notions, according to the different interests of their preachers.——There are very few amongst them (Achmet-beg denied there were any) so absurd, as to set up for wit, by declaring they believe no God at all. And Sir Paul Rycaut is mistaken (as he commonly is) in calling the sect Muterin (i. e. the secret with us) Atheists, they being Deists, whose impiety consists in making a jest of their prophet. Achmet-beg did not own to me, that he was of this opinion, but made no scruple of deviating from some part of Mahomet's law, by drinking wine with the same freedom we did. When I asked him how he came to allow himself that liberty; he made answer, that all the creatures of God are good, and designed for the use of man; however, that the prohibition of wine was a very wise maxim, and meant for the common people, being the source of all disorders amongst them: but that the prophet never designed to confine those that knew how to use it with moderation; nevertheless, he said that scandal ought to be avoided, and that he never drank it in public. This is the general way of thinking amongst them, and very few forbear drinking wine, that are able to afford it. He assured me, that

if

if I underſtood Arabic, I ſhould be very well pleaſed with reading the Alcoran, which is ſo far from the nonſenſe we charge it with, that 'tis the pureſt morality, delivered in the very beſt language. I have ſince heard impartial Chriſtians ſpeak of it in the ſame manner; and I don't doubt but that all our tranſlations are from copies got from the Greek prieſts, who would not fail to falſify it with the extremity of malice. No body of men ever were more ignorant, or more corrupt; yet they differ ſo little from the Romiſh church, that, I confeſs, nothing gives me a greater abhorrence of the cruelty of your clergy, than the barbarous perſecution of them, whenever they have been their maſters, for no other reaſon, than their not acknowledging the Pope. The diſſenting in that one article, has got them the titles of Heretics, and Schiſmatics; and what is worſe, the ſame treatment. I found at Philippopolis, a ſect of Chriſtians that call themſelves Paulines. They ſhew an old church, where, they ſay, St. Paul preached, and he is

their

their favourite Saint, after the same manner that St. Peter is at Rome; neither do they forget to give him the preference over the rest of the Apostles.

But of all the religions I have seen, that of the Arnounts seems to me the most particular; they are natives of Arnountlich, the ancient Macedonia, and still retain the courage and hardiness, though they have lost the name of Macedonians, being the best militia in the Turkish Empire, and the only check upon the Janizaries. They are foot soldiers; we had a guard of them, relieved in every considerable town we passed; they are all clothed and armed at their own expence, dressed in clean white coarse cloth, carrying guns of a prodigious length, which they run with on their shoulders, as if they did not feel the weight of them, the leader singing a sort of a rude tune, not unpleasant, and the rest making up the chorus. These people living between Christians and Mahometans, and not being skilled in controversy, declare, that they are utterly unable to judge

judge which religion is best; but to be certain of not entirely rejecting the truth, they very prudently follow both. They go to the mosques on Fridays, and to the church on Sunday,—saying for their excuse, that at the day of judgment they are sure of protection from the true prophet; but which that is, they are not able to determine in this world. I believe there is no other race of mankind, who have so modest an opinion of their own capacity.

These are the remarks I have made, on the diversity of religions I have seen. I don't ask your pardon for the liberty I have taken in speaking of the Roman. I know you equally condemn the quackery of all churches, as much as you revere the sacred truths, in which we both agree.

You will expect I should say something to you of the antiquities of this country, but there are few remains of ancient Greece. We passed near the piece of an arch which is commonly called

called Trajan's gate, from a suppofition that he made it to shut up the paffage over the mountains, between Sophia and Philippopolis. But I rather believe it the remains of some triumphal arch (though I could not see any inscription); for if that paffage had been shut up, there are many others that would serve for the march of an army; and notwithstanding the story of Baldwin Earl of Flanders being overthrown in thefe ftraits, after he won Conftantinople, I don't fancy the Germans would find themfelves ftopped by them at this day. 'Tis true, the road is now made (with great induftry) as commodious as poffible, for the march of the Turkish army; there is not one ditch or puddle between this place and Belgrade, that has not a large ftrong bridge of planks built over it; but the precipices are not fo terrible as I had heard them reprefented. At thefe mountains we lay at the little village Kifkoi, wholly inhabited by Chriftians, as all the peafants of Bulgaria are. Their houfes are nothing but little huts, raifed of dirt baked in the fun, sun, and they leave them and fly into the mountains, some months before the march of the Turkish army, who would else entirely ruin them, by driving away their whole flocks.— This precaution secures them in a sort of plenty; for such vast tracts of land lying in common, they have the liberty of sowing what they please, and are generally very industrious husbandmen. I drank here several sorts of delicious wine. The women dress themselves in a great variety of coloured glass beads, and are not ugly, but of tawney complexion. I have now told you all that is worth telling you, and perhaps more, relating to my journey. When I am at Constantinople, I'll try to pick up some curiosities, and then you shall hear again from

Yours, &c.

LETTER XXVIII.

To the Countess of B———.

Adrianople, April 1, O.S. 1717

AS I never can forget the smallest of your ladyship's commands, my first business here has been to enquire after the stuffs you ordered me to look for, without being able to find what you would like. The difference of the dress here and at London is so great, the same sort of things are not proper for *Caftans* and *Manteaus*. However, I will not give over my search, but renew it again at Constantinople, tho' I have reason to believe there is nothing finer than what is to be found here, as this place is at present the residence of the court. The Grand Signior's eldest daughter was married some few days before I came hither, and upon that occasion the Turkish ladies display all their magnificence. The bride was conducted to her husband's house in very great splendour.—

She

She is widow of the late Vizier, who was killed at Peterwaradin, though that ought rather to be called a contract than a marriage, since she never has lived with him; however, the greatest part of his wealth is hers. He had the permission of visiting her in the Seraglio; and being one of the handsomest men in the empire, had very much engaged her affections.—When she saw this second husband, who is at least fifty, she could not forbear bursting into tears. He is indeed a man of merit, and the declared favourite of the Sultan, (which they call *Mosayp*) but that is not enough to make him pleasing in the eyes of a girl of thirteen.

The government here is entirely in the hands of the army. The Grand Signior, with all his absolute power, is as much a slave as any of his subjects, and trembles at a Janizary's frown.——Here is, indeed, a much greater appearance of subjection than amongst us; a minister of state is not spoke to, but upon the knee; should a reflection on his conduct be dropt in a coffee-house, (for they have spies every

every where) the house would be raz'd to the ground, and perhaps the whole company put to the torture. No huzzaing mobs, senseless pamphlets, and tavern disputes about politics:

 A consequential ill that freedom draws;
 A bad effect—but from a noble cause.

None of our harmless calling names !—But when a minister here displeases the people, in three hours time he is dragged even from his master's arms. They cut off his hands, head, and feet, and throw them before the palace-gate, with all the respect in the world; while the Sultan (to whom they all profess an unlimited adoration) sits trembling in his apartment, and dare neither defend nor revenge his favourite. This is the blessed condition of the most absolute monarch upon earth, who owns no Law but his Will.

I cannot help wishing, in the loyalty of my heart, that the parliament would send hither a ship load of your passive obedient men, that they might see arbitrary government in its clearest strongest light, where 'tis hard to judge
          whether

whether the Prince, People, or Minifters, are moft miferable. I could make many reflections on this fubject; but I know, Madam, your own good fenfe has already furnifhed you with better than I am capable of.

I went yefterday along with the French Ambaffadrefs to fee the Grand Signior in his paffage to the Mofque. He was preceded by a numerous guard of Janizaries, with vaft white feathers on their heads, as alfo by the Spahis and Boftangees, (thefe are foot and horfeguards) and the Royal Gardeners, which are a very confiderable body of men, dreffed in different habits of fine lively colours, fo that at a diftance, they appeared like a parterre of tulips. After them the Aga of the Janizaries, in a robe of purple velvet, lined with filver tiffue, his horfe led by two flaves richly dreffed. Next him the Kyzlier Aga, (your lady knows, this is the chief guardian of the Seraglio Ladies) in a deep yellow cloth (which fuited very well to his black face) lined with fables. Laft came his Sublimity himfelf, arrayed in green,

lined

lined with the fur of a black Muscovite fox, which is supposed to be worth a thousand pounds sterling, and mounted on a fine horse, with furniture embroidered with jewels. Six more horses, richly comparisoned, were led by him; and two of his principal courtiers bore, one his gold, and the other his silver coffee-pot, on a staff; another carried a silver stool on his head for him to sit on.—It would be too tedious to tell your ladyship the various dresses and turbants by which their rank is distinguished; but they were all extremely rich and gay, to the number of some thousands; so that perhaps there cannot be seen a more beautiful procession. The Sultan appeared to us a handsome man of about forty, with something, however, severe in his countenance, and his eyes very full and black. He happened to stop under the window where we stood, and (I suppose being told who we were) looked upon us very attentively, so that we had full leisure to consider him. The French Ambassadress agreed with me as to his good mien. I see that lady

lady very often; she is young, and her conversation would be a great relief to me, if I could persuade her to live without those forms and ceremonies that make life formal and tiresome. But she is so delighted with her guards, her four-and-twenty footmen, gentlemen-ushers, &c. that she would rather die than make me a visit without them; not to reckon a coachful of attending damsels yclep'd maids of honour. What vexes me is, that as long as she will visit me with a troublesome equipage, I am obliged to do the same; however, our mutual interest makes us much together. I went with her the other day all round the town, in an open gilt chariot, with our joint train of attendants, preceded by our guards, who might have summoned the people to see what they had never seen, nor ever perhaps would see again, two young Christian Ambassadresses at the same time. Your ladyship may easily imagine, we drew a vast croud of spectators, but all silent as death. If any of them had taken the liberties of our mobs upon any strange sight, our Janizaries

zaries had made no scruple of falling on them with their scymitars, without danger for so doing, being above law. These people however (I mean the Janizaries) have some good qualities; they are very zealous and faithful where they serve, and look upon it as their business to fight for you on all occasions. Of this I had a very pleasant instance in a village on this side Philippopolis, where we were met by our domestic guards. I happened to bespeak pigeons for supper, upon which one of my Janizaries went immediately to the Cadi (the chief civil officer of the town) and ordered him to send in some dozens. The poor man answered, that he had already sent about, but could get none. My Janizary, in the height of his zeal for my service, immediately locked him up prisoner in his room, telling him he deserved death for his impudence, in offering to excuse his not obeying my command; but, out of respect to me, he would not punish him but by my order. Accordingly he came very gravely to me, to ask what should be done to him; adding, by way of compliment, that if I pleafed he would bring me his head.———This may give you fome idea of the unlimited power of thefe fellows, who are all fworn brothers, and bound to revenge the injuries done to one another, whether at Cairo, Aleppo, or any part of the world. This inviolable league makes them fo powerful, that the greateft man at court never fpeaks to them but in a flattering tone; and in Afia, any man that is rich, is forced to enroll himfelf a Janizary to fecure his eftate.—But I have already faid enough, and I dare fwear, dear Madam, that, by this time, 'tis a very comfortable reflection to you, that there is no poffibility of your receiving fuch a tedious letter but once in fix months; 'tis that confideration has given me the affurance of entertaining you fo long, and will, I hope, plead the excufe of, dear Madam,

Your's, &c.

LETTER XXIX.

To the Countess of ————

Adrianople, April 1, O.S. 1717.

I WISH to God, dear sister, that you were as regular in letting me know what passes on your side of the globe, as I am careful in endeavouring to amuse you by the account of all I see here, that I think worth your notice. You content yourself with telling me over and over that the town is very dull: it may possibly be dull to you, when every day does not present you with something new; but for me, that am in arrears, at least two months news, all that seems very stale with you, would be very fresh and sweet here. Pray let me into more particulars, and I will try to awaken your gratitude by giving you a full and true relation of the novelties of this place, none of which would surprize you more than a sight of my person, as I am now in my Turkish habit, though I believe you would be of my opinion,

nion, that 'tis admirably becoming.—I intend to send you my picture; in the mean time accept of it here.

The first part of my dress is a pair of drawers, very full, that reach to my shoes, and conceal the legs more modestly than your petticoats. They are of a thin rose-coloured damask, brocaded with silver flowers. My shoes are of a white kid leather, embroidered with gold. Over this hangs my smock, of a fine white silk gauze, edged with embroidery. This smock has wide sleeves hanging half-way down the arm, and is closed at the neck with a diamond button, but the shape and colour of the bosom is very well to be distinguished through it.—The Antery is a waistcoat, made close to the shape, of white and gold damask, with very long sleeves falling back, and fringed with deep gold fringe, and should have diamond or pearl buttons. My Caftan, of the same stuff with my drawers, is a robe exactly fitted to my shape and reaching to my feet, with very long strait falling sleeves. Over this is the girdle,

girdle, of about four fingers broad, which all that can afford it, have entirely of diamonds or other precious stones; those, who will not be at that expence, have it of exquisite embroidery on fattin; but it must be fastened before with a clasp of diamonds.—The *Curdée* is a loose robe they throw off, or put on, according to the weather, being of a rich brocade (mine is green and gold) either lined with ermine or sables; the sleeves reach very little below the shoulders. The head-dress is composed of a cap called Talpock, which is, in winter, of fine velvet embroidered with pearls or diamonds, and, in summer, of a light shining silver stuff. This is fixed on one side of the head, hanging a little way down with a gold tassel, and bound on, either with a circle of diamonds (as I have seen several) or a rich embroidered handkerchief. On the other side of the head the hair is laid flat; and here the ladies are at liberty to shew their fancies; some putting flowers, others a plume of heron's feathers, and, in short, what they please; but the most

general

general fashion is, a large Bouquet of jewels, made like natural flowers, that is, the buds of pearl; the roses of different coloured rubies; the jessamines of diamonds; the jonquils of topazes, &c. so well set and enamelled, 'tis hard to imagine any thing of that kind so beau-. tiful. The hair hangs at its full length behind, divided into tresses braided with pearl or ribbon, which is always in great quantity. I never saw in my life, so many fine heads of hair. In one lady's I have counted a hundred and ten of the tresses, all natural; but it must be owned that every kind of beauty is more common here than with us. 'Tis surprizing to see a young woman that is not very handsome. They have naturally the most beautiful complexion in the world, and generally large black eyes. I can assure you with great truth, that the court of England (though I believe it the fairest in Christendom) does not contain so many beauties as are under our protection here. They generally shape their eye-brows, and, both Greeks and Turks have the custom of

putting

putting round their eyes a black tincture, that, at a distance, or by candle-light, adds very much to the blackness of them. I fancy many of our ladies would be overjoyed to know this secret; but 'tis too visible by day. They dye their nails a rose colour; but, I own, I cannot enough accustom myself to this fashion, to find any beauty in it.

As to their morality or good conduct, I can say, like Harlequin, that 'tis just as 'tis with you; and the Turkish ladies don't commit one sin the less for not being Christians. Now that I am a little acquainted with their ways, I cannot forbear admiring, either exemplary discretion, or extreme stupidity of all the writers that have given accounts of them. 'Tis very easy to see, they have in reality more liberty than we have. No woman, of what rank soever, is permitted to go into the streets without two *Murlins*, one that covers her face, all but her eyes; and another, that hides the whole dress of her head, and hangs half way down her back. Their shapes are also wholly concealed by a thing they call a *Ferigée*, which no woman of any

sort

fort appears without; this has ſtrait ſleeves, that reach to their fingers ends, and it laps all round them, not unlike a riding-hood. In winter, 'tis of cloth; and in ſummer, of plain ſtuff or ſilk. You may gueſs then how effectually this diſguiſes them, ſo that there is no diſtinguiſhing the great lady from her ſlave. 'Tis impoſſible for the moſt jealous huſband to know his wife, when he meets her, and no man dare touch or follow a woman in the ſtreet.

This perpetual maſquerade gives them entire liberty of following their inclinations without danger of diſcovery. The moſt uſual method of intrigue is, to ſend an appointment to the lover to meet the lady at a Jew's ſhop, which are as notoriouſly convenient as our Indian houſes; and yet, even thoſe who don't make uſe of them, do not ſcruple to go to buy penny-worths, and tumble over rich goods, which are chiefly to be found amongſt that ſort of people. The great ladies ſeldom let their gallants know who they are; and 'tis ſo difficult to find it out, that they can very ſeldom gueſs at her name, whom they have correſponded
with

with for above half a year together. You may eafily imagine the number of faithful wives very fmall in a country where they have nothing to fear from a lover's indifcretion, fince we fee fo many have the courage to expofe themfelves to that in this world, and all the threatened punifhment of the next, which is never preached to the Turkifh damfels. Neither have they much to apprehend from the refentment of their hufbands: thofe ladies that are rich, having all their money in their own hands. Upon the whole, I look upon the Turkifh women, as the only free people in the Empire; the very Divan pays a refpect to them, and the Grand Signior himfelf, when a Baffa is executed, never violates the privileges of the Haram, (or womens apartment) which remains unfearched and entire to the widow. They are Queens of their flaves, whom the hufband has no permiffion fo much as to look upon, except it be an old woman or two that his lady chufes. 'Tis true, their law permits them four wives, but there is no inftance of a man of quality that

makes

makes use of this liberty, or of a woman of rank that would suffer it. When a husband happens to be inconstant (as those things will happen) he keeps his mistress in a house apart, and visits her as privately as he can, just as 'tis with you. Amongst all the great men here, I only know the Tefterdar (i. e. Treasurer) that keeps a number of she-slaves for his own use, (that is, on his own side of the house, for a slave once given to serve a lady, is entirely at her disposal) and he is spoke of as a libertine, or what we should call a rake; and his wife won't see him; though she continues to live in his house. Thus you see, dear sister, the manners, of mankind do not differ so widely, as our voyage writers would make us believe. Perhaps, it would be more entertaining to add a few surprising customs of my own invention; but nothing seems to me so agreeable as truth, and I believe nothing so acceptable to you. I conclude therefore, with repeating the great truth of my being,

Dear Sister, &c.

LETTER XXX.

To Mr. Pope.

Adrianople, April 1, O. S.

I DARE say you expect, at least, something very new in this letter, after I have gone a journey, not undertaken, by any Christian, for some hundred years. The most remarkable accident that happened to me, was my being very near over-turned into the Hebrus; and, if I had much regard for the glories that one's name enjoys after death, I should certainly be sorry for having missed the romantic conclusion of swimming down the same river in which the musical head of Orpheus repeated verses, so many ages since:

"*Caput a cervice revulsum,*
"*Gurdite cum medio, portans Oeagrius Hebrus*
"*Volveret, Euridicen vox ipsa, et frigida lingua*
"*Ah! miseram Euridicen! anima fugiente vocabat,*
"*Euridicen toto referebant flumine ripæ.*"

Who knows but some of your right wits might have found it a subject affording many

poetical

poetical turns, and have told the world in an heroic Elegy, that,

As equal were our souls, so equal were our fates.

I despair of ever hearing so many fine things said of me, as so extraordinary a death would have given occasion for.

I am at this present moment writing in a house situated on the banks of the Hebrus, which runs under my chamber window. My garden is full of tall cypress trees, upon the branches of which, several couple of true turtles are saying soft things to one another from morning till night. How naturally do *boughs* and *vows* come into my mind, at this minute? And must not you confess, to my praise, that 'tis more than an ordinary discretion, that can resist the wicked suggestions of poetry, in a place where truth, for once, furnishes all the ideas of pastoral. The summer is already far advanced, in this part of the world; and for some miles round Adrianople, the whole ground is

laid

laid out in gardens, and the banks of the rivers are set with rows of fruit trees, under which all the most considerable Turks divert themselves every evening, not with walking, that is not one of their pleasures; but a set party of them choose out a green spot, where the shade is very thick, and there they spread a carpet, on which they sit drinking their coffee, and are generally attended by some slave with a fine voice, or that plays on some instrument. Every twenty paces you may see one of these little companies, listening to the dashing of the river; and this taste is so universal, that the very gardeners are not without it. I have often seen them and their children sitting on the banks of the river, and playing on a rural instrument, perfectly answering the description of the ancient Fistula, being composed of unequal reeds, with a simple but agreeable softness in the sound.

Mr. Addison might here make the experiment he speaks of in his travels; there not being one instrument of music among the Greek or Roman

man statues, that is not to be found in the hands of the people of this country. The young lads generally divert themselves with making garlands for their favourite lambs, which I have often seen painted and adorned with flowers, lying at their feet, while they sung or played. It is not that they ever read Romances. But these are the ancient amusements here, and as natural to them as cudgel-playing and foot-ball to our British swains; the softness and warmth of the climate forbidding all rough exercises, which were never so much as heard of amongst them, and naturally inspiring a laziness and aversion to labour, which the great plenty indulges. These gardeners are the only happy race of country people in Turkey. They furnish all the city with fruits and herbs, and seem to live very easily. They are most of them Greeks, and have little houses in the midst of their gardens, where their wives and daughters take a liberty, not permitted in the town, I mean to go unveiled. These wenches are very neat and handsome,

handsome, and pass their time at their looms under the trees.

I no longer look upon Theocritus as a romantic writer; he has only given a plain image of the way of life amongst the peasants of his country, who, before oppression had reduced them to want, were, I suppose, all employed as the better sort of them are now. I don't doubt, had he been born a Briton, but his Idylliums had been filled with descriptions of threshing and churning, both which are unknown here, the corn being all trod out by oxen; and butter (I speak it with sorrow) unheard of.

I read over your Homer here with an infinite pleasure, and find several little passages explained, 'that I did not before entirely comprehend the beauty of: Many of the customs, and much of the dress then in fashion, being yet retained. I don't wonder to find more remains here, of an age so distant, than is to be found in any other country, the Turks not taking that pains to introduce their own manners,

ners, as has been generally practised by other nations, that imagine themselves more polite. It would be too tedious to you to point out all the passages that relate to present customs. But I can assure you, that the Princesses and great ladies pass their time at their looms, embroidering veils and robes, surrounded by their maids, which are always very numerous, in the same manner as we find Andromache and Helen described. The description of the belt of Menelaus exactly resembles those that are now worn by the great men, fastened before with broad golden clasps, and embroidered round with rich work. The snowy veil, that Helen throws over her face, is still fashionable; and I never see half a dozen of old Bashaws (as I do very often) with their reverend beards, sitting basking in the sun, but I recollect good King Priam and his counsellors. Their manner of dancing is certainly the same that Diana is *sung* to have danced on the banks of Eurotas. The great lady still leads the dance, and is followed by a troop of young girls, who imitate her steps, and if she sings, make up the chorus. The tunes are extremely gay and lively, yet with something in them wonderfully soft. The steps are varied according to the pleasure of her that leads the dance, but always in exact time, and infinitely more agreeable than any of our dances, at least in my opinion. I sometimes make one in the train, but am not skilful enough to lead; these are the Grecian dances, the Turkish being very different.

I should have told you, in the first place, that the Eastern manners give a great light into many scripture passages, that appear odd to us, their phrases being commonly what we should call Scripture language. The vulgar Turk is very different from what is spoke at court, or amongst the people of figure; who always mix so much Arabic and Persian in their discourse, that it may very well be called another language. And 'tis as ridiculous to make use of the expressions commonly used, in speaking to a great man or lady, as it would be

to

to speak broad Yorkshire, or Somersetshire, in the drawing-room. Besides this distinction, they have what they call the sublime, that is, a stile proper for poetry, and which is the exact Scripture stile. I believe you would be pleased to see a genuine example of this; and I am very glad I have it in my power to satisfy your curiosity, by sending you a faithful copy of the verses that Ibrahim Bassa, the reigning favourite, has made for the young Princess, his contracted wife, whom he is not yet permitted to visit without witnesses, though she is gone home to his house. He is a man of wit and learning; and whether or no he is capable of writing good verse, you may be sure that, on such an occasion, he would not want the assistance of the best poets in the empire. Thus the verses may be looked upon as a sample of their finest poetry, and I don't doubt you'll be of my mind, that it is most wonderfully resembling the Song of Solomon, which also was addressed to a Royal Bride.

TURKISH VERSES addressed to the SULTANA, eldest daughter of SULTAN ACHMET III.

STANZA I.

Ver. *The nightingale now wanders in the vines;*
1,   *Her passion is to seek roses.*

2. *I went down to admire the beauty of the vines;*
   The sweetness of your charms has ravish'd my soul.

3. *Your eyes are black and lovely,*
   But wild and disdainful as those of a stag;

STANZA II.

1. *The wished possession is delayed from day to day,*
   The cruel Sultan ACHMET *will not permit me*
   To see those cheeks more vermillion than roses.

2. *I dare not snatch one of your kisses,*
   The sweetness of your charms has ravish'd my soul.

3. *Your eyes are black and lovely,*
   But wild and disdainful as those of a stag.

STANZA III.

1. *The wretched* IBRAHIM *sighs in these verses,*
   One dart from your eyes has pierc'd thro' my heart.

2. *Ah!*

2. *Ah! when will the hour of possession arrive?*
    Must I yet wait a long time?
    The sweetness of your charms has ravish'd my soul.

3. *Ah!* SULTANA! *stag-ey'd—an angel amongst angels!*
    I desire, and, *my desire remains unsatisfied.*
    Can you take delight to prey upon my heart?

STANZA IV.

1. *My cries pierce the heavens!*
    My eyes are without sleep!
    Turn to me, SULTANA——*let me gaze on thy beauty.*

2. *Adieu———I go down to the grave.*
    If you call me———I return.
    My heart is——hot as sulphur;——sigh and it will flame.

3. *Crown of my life, fair light of my eyes!*
    My SULTANA! *my princess!*
    I rub my face against the earth;---I am drown'd in scalding tears---I rave!
    Have you no compassion? will you not turn to look upon me?

I have

I have taken abundance of pains to get these verses in a literal translation; and if you were acquainted with my interpreters, I might spare myself the trouble of assuring you, that they have received no poetical touches from their hands. In my opinion, (allowing for the inevitable faults of a prose translation into a language so very different) there is a good deal of beauty in them. The epithet of "stag-ey'd," (though the sound is not very agreeable in English) pleases me extremely; and I think it a very lively image of the fire and indifference in his mistress's eyes.—Monsieur Boileau has very justly observed, that we are never to judge of the elevation of an expression in an antient author by the sound it carries with us; since it may be extremely fine with them, when, at the same time, it appears low or uncouth to us. You are so well acquainted with Homer, you cannot but have observed the same thing, and you must have the same indulgence for all oriental poetry. The repetitions at the end of the two first stanzas are meant for a sort of Chorus,

and

and are agreeable to the antient manner of writing. The music of the verses apparently changes in the third Stanza, where the burden is altered; and I think he very artfully seems more passionate at the conclusion, as 'tis natural for people to warm themselves by their own discourse, especially on a subject in which one is deeply concerned; 'tis certainly far more touching, than our modern custom of concluding a song of passion, with a turn which is inconsistent with it. The first verse is a description of the season of the year; all the country now being full of Nightingales, whose amours with roses, is an Arabian fable, as well known here, as any part of Ovid amongst us, and is much the same as if an English poem should begin, by saying,—" Now Philomela sings." Or what if I turned the whole into the stile of English poetry, to see how it would look?

STANZA I.

NOW Philomel renews her tender strain,
Indulging all the night her pleasing pain;

I sought the groves to hear the wanton sing,
There saw a face more beauteous than the spring.

Your large stag-eyes where thousand glories play
As bright, as lively, but as wild as they.

STANZA II.

In vain I'm promis'd such a heavenly prize.
Ah! cruel SULTAN! who delay'st my joys!
While piercing charms transfix my amorous heart,
I dare not snatch one kiss, to ease the smart.
Those eyes like, &c.

STANZA III.

Your wretched lover in these lines complains;
From those dear beauties rise his killing pains.

When will the hour of wish'd-for bliss arrive,
Must I wait longer? Can I wait and live?

Ah! bright SULTANA! maid divinely fair!
Can you, unpitying, see the pains I bear?

STANZA IV.

The Heavens relenting hear my piercing cries,
I loath the light, and sleep forsakes my eyes,
Turn thee, SULTANA, ere thy lover dies;

Sinking

Sinking to earth, I sigh the last adieu,
Call me, my Goddess, and my life renew.

My Queen! my angel! my fond heart's desire!
I rave,—my bosom burns with heavenly fire!
Pity that passion which thy charms inspire.

   I have taken the liberty in the second verse, of following what I suppose the true sense of the author, though not literally expressed. By his saying he went down to admire the beauty of the vines, and her charms ravished his soul; I understand a poetical fiction, of having first seen her in a garden, where he was admiring the beauty of the spring. But I could not forbear retaining the comparison of her eyes with those of a stag, though perhaps the novelty of it may give it a burlesque sound in our language. I cannot determine upon the whole, how well I have succeeded in the translation, neither do I think our English proper to express such violence of passion, which is very seldom felt amongst us. We want, also, those compound words which are very frequent and strong in the Turkish language.

You see I am pretty far gone in oriental learning, and to say truth, I study very hard. I wish my studies may give me an occasion of entertaining your curiosity, which will be the utmost advantage hoped for from them, by,

Your's, &c.

LETTER XXXI.

To Mrs. S. C.

Adrianople, April 1, O. S.

IN my opinion, dear S. I ought rather to quarrel with you, for not answering my Nimuegen letter of August, till December, than to excuse my not writing again till now. I am sure there is on my side a very good excuse for silence, having gone such tiresome land-journies, though I don't find the conclusion of them so bad as you seem to imagine. I am very easy here, and not in the solitude you fancy me. The great number of Greeks, French, English, and Italians, that are under our protection, make their court to me from morning till night; and I'll assure you, are, many of them, very fine ladies; for there is no possibility for a Christian to live easily under this government, but by the protection of an Ambassador——and the richer they are, the greater is their danger.

Those dreadful stories you have heard of the plague, have very little foundation in truth. I own, I have much ado to reconcile myself to the sound of a word, which has always given me such terrible ideas; though I am convinced there is little more in it, than in a fever. As a proof of this, let me tell you, that we passed through two or three towns most violently infected. In the very next house where we lay (in one of those places) two persons died of it. Luckily for me, I was so well deceived, that I knew nothing of the matter; and I was made believe, that our second cook had only a great cold. However, we left our doctor to take care of him, and yesterday they both arrived here in good health; and I am now let into the secret, that he has had the plague. There are many that escape it, neither is the air ever infected. I am persuaded that it would be as easy a matter to root it out here, as out of Italy and France; but it does so little mischief, they are not very solicitous about it, and are content to

suffer

suffer this distemper, instead of our variety, which they are utterly unacquainted with.

A propos of distempers, I am going to tell you a thing, that will make you wish yourself here. The small pox, so fatal, and so general amongst us, is here intirely harmless, by the invention of engrafting, which is the term they give it. There is a set of old women, who make it their business to perform the operation, every autumn, in the month of September, when the great heat is abated. People send to one another to know if any of their family has a mind to have the small-pox; they make parties for this purpose, and when they are met (commonly fifteen or sixteen together) the old woman comes with a nut-shell full of the matter of the best sort of small-pox, and asks what vein you please to have opened. She immediately rips open that, you offer to her, with a large needle, (which gives you no more pain than a common scratch) and puts into the vein as much matter as can lie upon the head of her needle, and after that, binds up the little wound with a

hollow

hollow bit of shell, and in this manner opens four or five veins. The Grecians have commonly the superstition of opening one in the middle of the forehead, one in each arm, and one on the breast, to mark the sign of the cross; but this has a very ill effect, all these wounds leaving little scars, and is not done by those that are not superstitious, who chuse to have them in the legs, or that part of the arm that is concealed. The children or young patients play together all the rest of the day, and are in perfect health to the eighth. Then the fever begins to seize them, and they keep their beds two days, very seldom three. They have very rarely above twenty or thirty in their faces, which never mark, and in eight days time they are as well as before their illness. Where they are wounded, there remains running sores during the distemper, which I don't doubt is a great relief to it. Every year thousands undergo this operation, and the French Ambassador says pleasantly, that they take the smallpox here by way of diversion, as they take

the

the waters in other countries. There is no example of any one that has died in it, and you may believe I am well satisfied of the safety of this experiment, since I intend to try it on my dear little son. I am patriot enough to take pains to bring this useful invention into fashion in England, and I should not fail to write to some of our doctors very particularly about it, if I knew any one of them that I thought had virtue enough to destroy such a considerable branch of their revenue, for the good of mankind. But that distemper is too beneficial to them, not to expose to all their resentment, the hardy wight that should undertake to put an end to it. Perhaps if I live to return I may, however, have courage to war with them. Upon this occasion, admire the heroism in the heart of,

Your friend, &c. &c.

LETTER XXXII.

To Mrs. T.

Adrianople, April 1, O.S. 1718.

I CAN now tell dear Mrs. T——, that I am safely arrived at the end of my very long journey. I will not tire you with the account of the many fatigues I have suffered. You would rather be informed of the strange things that are to be seen here; and a letter out of Turkey, that has nothing extraordinary in it, would be as great a disappointment as my visitors will receive at London, if I return thither without any rarities to shew them.— What shall I tell you of?——You never saw camels in your life; and perhaps the description of them will appear new to you; I can assure you, the first sight of them was so to me; and though I have seen hundreds of pictures of those animals, I never saw any that was resembling enough to give a true idea of them. I am going to make a bold observation, and possibly

possibly a false one, because nobody has ever made it before me; but I do take them to be of the stag-kind; their legs, bodies, and necks, are exactly shaped like them, and their colour very near the same. 'Tis true, they are much larger, being a great deal higher than a horse, and so swift, that, after the defeat of Peterwaradin, they far outran the swiftest horses, and brought the first news of the loss of the battle to Belgrade. They are never thoroughly tamed; the drivers take care to tye them one to another with strong ropes, fifty in a string, led by an ass, on which the driver rides. I have seen three hundred in one caravan. They carry the third part more than a horse; but 'tis a particular art to load them, because of the bunch of their backs. They seem to me very ugly creatures, their heads being ill formed and disproportioned to their bodies. They carry all the burdens; and the beasts destined to the plough are buffaloes, an animal also you are unacquainted with. They are larger and more clumsy than an ox; they have

have short thick black horns close to their heads, which grow turning backwards. They say this horn looks very beautiful when 'tis well polished. They are all black, with very short hair on their hides, and have extremely little white eyes, that make them look like devils. The country people dye their tails, and the hair of their forehead red, by way of ornament. Horses are not put here to any laborious work, nor are they at all fit for it. They are beautiful and full of spirit, but generally little, and not strong, as the breed of colder countries; very gentle, however, with all their vivacity, and also swift and sure-footed. I have a little white favourite, that I would not part with on any terms; he prances under me with so much fire, you would think that I had a great deal of courage to dare mount him; yet I'll assure you I never rid a horse so much at my command, in my life. My side-saddle is the first that was ever seen in this part of the world, and is gazed at with as much wonder as the ship of Columbus in the

first

first discovery of America. Here are some little birds, held in a sort of religious reverence, and for that reason multiply prodigiously; Turtles on the account of their innocence; and Storks, because they are supposed to make every winter the pilgrimage to Mecca. To say truth, they are the happiest subjects under the Turkish government, and are so sensible of their privileges, that they walk the streets without fear, and generally build in the low parts of houses. Happy are those whose houses are so distinguished, as the vulgar Turks are perfectly persuaded, that they will not be, that year, attacked either by fire or pestilence. I have the happiness of one of their sacred nests under my chamber window.

Now I am talking of my chamber, I remember, the description of the houses here will be as new to you, as any of the birds or beasts. I suppose you have read in most of our accounts of Turkey, that their houses are the most miserable pieces of building in the world. I can speak very learnedly on that subject, having been in so many of them; and I assure you, 'tis no such thing. We are now lodged in a palace, belonging to the Grand Signior. I really think the manner of building here very agreeable, and proper for the country. 'Tis true, they are not, at all, solicitous to beautify the outsides of their houses, and they are generally built with wood, which, I own, is the cause of many inconveniences; but this is not to be charged on the ill taste of the people, but on the oppression of the government. Every house at the death of its master, is at the Grand Signior's disposal, and therefore no man cares to make a great expence, which he is not sure his family will be the better for. . All their design is to build a house commodious and that will last their lives; and they are very different if it falls down the year after. Every house, great and small, is divided into two distinct parts, which only join together by a narrow passage. The first house has a large court before it, and open galleries all round it, which is, to me, a thing very

very agreeable. This gallery leads to all the chambers, which are commonly large, and with two rows of windows, the firſt being of painted glaſs; they ſeldom build above two ſtories, each of which has galleries. The ſtairs are broad, and not often above thirty ſteps. This is the houſe belonging to the lord, and the adjoining one is called the Haram, that is, the ladies' apartment, (for the name of ſeraglio is peculiar to the Grand Signior;) it has alſo a gallery running round it towards the garden, to which all the windows are turned, and the ſame number of chambers as the other, but more gay and ſplendid, both in painting and furniture. The ſecond row of windows are very low, with grates like thoſe of convents, the rooms are all ſpread with Perſian carpets, and raiſed at one end of them (my chambers are raiſed at both ends) about two feet. This is the Sopha, which is laid with a richer ſort of carpet, and all round it a ſort of couch raiſed half a foot, covered with rich ſilk according to the fancy or magnificence of the owner. Mine is of scarlet cloth with a gold fringe; round about this are placed, standing against the wall, two rows of cushions, the first very large, and the rest little ones; and here the Turks display their greatest magnificence. They are generally brocade, or embroidery of gold wire upon white sattin.—Nothing can look more gay and splendid.—These seats are also so convenient and easy, that I believe I shall never endure chairs as long as I live—The rooms are low, which I think no fault, and the cieling is always of wood, generally inlaid or painted with flowers. They open in many places with folding doors, and serve for cabinets, I think more conveniently than ours. Between the windows are little arches to set pots of perfume, or baskets of flowers. But what pleases me best, is the fashion of having marble fountains in the lower part of the room, which throw up several spouts of water, giving, at the same time an agreeable coolness, and a pleasant dashing sound, falling from one bason to another. Some of these are very magnificent.

Each

Each house has a bagnio, which consists generally in two or three little rooms leaded on the top, paved with marble, with basons, cocks of water, and all conveniencies for either hot or cold baths.

You will perhaps be surprised at an account so different from what you have been entertained with by the common voyage-writers, who are very fond of speaking of what they don't know. It must be under a very particular character, or on some extraordinary occasion, that a Christian is admitted into the house of a man of quality, and their Harams are always forbidden ground. Thus they can only speak of the outside, which makes no great appearance; and the womens apartments are always built backward, removed from sight, and have no other prospect than the gardens, which are inclosed with very high walls. There is none of our parterres in them; but they are planted with high trees, which give an agreeable shade, and, to my fancy, a pleasing view. In the midst of the garden is the Chiosk, that is, a

large

large room, commonly beautified with a fine fountain in the midst of it. It is raised nine or ten steps, and enclosed with gilded lattices, round which, vines, jessamines, and honey-suckles, make a sort of green wall. Large trees are planted round this place, which is the scene of their greatest pleasures, and where the ladies spend most of their hours, employed by their musick or embroidery.— In the public gardens, there are public Chiosks, where people go that are not so well accommodated at home, and drink their coffee, sherbet, &c. Neither are they ignorant of a more durable manner of building; their mosques are all of free-stone, and the public Hanns, or Inns, extremely magnificent, many of them taking up a large square, built round with shops under stone arches, where poor artificers are lodged gratis. They have always a mosque joining to them, and the body of the Hann is a most noble hall, capable of holding three or four hundred persons, the court extremely spacious, and cloisters round it, it, that give it the air of our colleges. I own, I think it a more reasonable piece of charity than the founding of convents.—I think I have now told you a great deal for once. If you don't like my choice of subjects, tell me what you would have me write upon; there is nobody more desirous to entertain you than, dear Mrs. T.

Yours, &c. &c.

LETTER XXXIII.

To the Countefs of ————

Adrianople, April 18, O. S.

I WROTE to you, dear fifter, and to all my other Englifh correfpondents, by the laft fhip, and only Heaven can tell, when I fhall have another opportunity of fending to you; but I cannot forbear to write again, though perhaps my letter may lye upon my hands thefe two months. To confefs the truth, my head is fo full of my entertainment yefterday, that 'tis abfolutely neceffary, for my own repofe, to give it fome vent. Without farther preface I will then begin my ftory.

I was invited to dine with the Grand Vizier's lady, and it was with a great deal of pleafure I prepared myfelf for an entertainment, which was never before given to any Chriftian. I thought I fhould very little fatisfy her curiofity, (which I did not doubt was a confiderable motive to the invitation) by going in a drefs fhe

was

was used to see, and therefore dressed myself in the court habit of Vienna, which is much more magnificent than ours. However, I chose to go *incognito*, to avoid any disputes about ceremony, and went in a Turkish coach only attended by my woman, that held up my train, and the Greek lady, who was my interpretess. I was met, at the court door, by her black Eunuch, who helped me out of the coach with great respect, and conducted me through several rooms, where her she slaves, finely dressed, were ranged on each side. In the innermost, I found the lady sitting on her sofa, in a sable vest. She advanced to meet me, and presented me half a dozen of her friends, with great civility. She seemed a very good woman, near fifty years old. I was surprised to observe so little magnificence in her house, the furniture being all very moderate; and, except the habits and number of her slaves, nothing about her appeared expensive. She guessed at my thoughts, and told me, she was no longer of an age to spend

either

either her time or money in superfluities; that her whole expence was in charity, and her whole employment praying to God. There was no affectation in this speech; both she and her husband are entirely given up to devotion. He never looks upon any other woman; and what is much more extraordinary, touches no bribes, notwithstanding the example of all his predecessors. He is so scrupulous in this point, he would not accept Mr. W———'s present, till he had been assured over and over, that it was a settled perquisite of his place, at the entrance of every Ambassador. She entertained me with all kind of civility, till dinner came in, which was served, one dish at a time, to a vast number, all finely dressed after their manner, which I don't think so bad as you have perhaps heard it represented. I am a very good judge of their eating, having lived three weeks in the house of an Effendi at Belgrade, who gave us very magnificent dinners, dressed by his own cooks. The first week they pleased me extremely; but, I own, I then begun to grow

weary

weary of their table, and defired our own cook might add a difh or two after our manner. But I attribute this to cuftom, and am very much inclined to believe, that an Indian who had never tafted of either, would prefer their cookery to ours. Their fauces are very high, all the roaft very much done. They ufe a great deal of very rich fpice. The foup is ferved for the laft difh; and they have, at leaft, as great a variety of ragouts, as we have. I was very forry I could not eat of as many as the good lady would have had me, who was very earneft in ferving me of every thing. The treat concluded with coffee and perfumes, which is a high mark of refpect; two flaves kneeling cenfed my hair, clothes, and handkerchief. After this ceremony, fhe commanded her flaves to play and dance, which they did with their guitars in their hands, and fhe excufed to me their want of fkill, faying fhe took no care to accomplifh them in that art.

I returned her thanks, and foon after took my leave. I was conducted back in the fame

manner

manner I entered, and would have gone strait to my own house, but the Greek lady, with me, earnestly sollicited me to visit the Kahya's lady, saying, he was the second officer in the Empire, and ought indeed to be looked upon as the first, the Grand Vizier having only the name, while he exercised the authority. I had found so little diversion in the Vizier's Haram, that I had no mind to go into another. But her importunity prevailed with me, and I am extremely glad, I was so complaisant. All things here were with quite another air than at the Grand Vizier's; and the very house confessed the difference between an old devotee, and a young beauty. It was nicely clean and magnificent. I was met at the door by two black Eunuchs, who led me through a long gallery, between two ranks of beautiful young girls, with their hair finely plaited, almost hanging to their feet, and dressed in fine light damasks, brocaded with silver. I was sorry that decency did not permit me to stop to consider them nearer. But that thought was

lost

lost upon my entrance into a large room, or rather pavillion, built round with gilded sashes, which were most of them thrown up, and the trees planted near them gave an agreeable shade, which hindered the sun from being troublesome. The jessamines and honey-suckles that twisted round their trunks, shed a soft perfume, increased by a white marble fountain playing sweet water in the lower part of the room, which fell into three or four basons, with a pleasing sound. The roof was painted with all sorts of flowers, falling out of gilded baskets, that seemed tumbling down. On a sofa, raised three steps, and covered with fine Persian carpets, sat the Kahya's lady, leaning on cushions of white sattin embroidered; and at her feet sat two young girls about twelve years old, lovely as angels, dressed perfectly rich, and almost covered with jewels. But they were hardly seen near the fair Fatima, (for that is her name) so much her beauty effaced every thing I have seen, nay, all that has been called lovely, either in England or Germany.

many. I muſt own, that I never ſaw any thing ſo glorioully beautiful, nor can I recollect a face that would have been taken notice of near her's. She ſtood up to receive me, ſaluting me, after their faſhion, putting her hand to her heart with a ſweetneſs full of majeſty, that no court breeding could ever give. She ordered cuſhions to be given me, and took care to place me in the corner, which is the place of honour. I confeſs, though the Greek lady had before given me a great opinion of her beauty, I was ſo ſtruck with admiration, that I could not, for ſome time, ſpeak to her, being wholly taken up in gazing. That ſurprizing harmony of features! That charming reſult of the whole! That exact proportion of body! That lovely bloom of complexion unſullied by art! The unutterable enchantment of her ſmile;—But her eyes!——Large and black, with all the ſoft languiſhment of the blue! every turn of her face diſcovering ſome new grace.

After

After my first surprize was over, I endeavoured by nicely examining her face, to find out some imperfection, without any fruit of my search, but my being clearly convinced of the error of that vulgar notion, that a face exactly proportioned, and perfectly beautiful, would not be agreeable; nature having done for her, with more success, what Apelles is said to have essayed by a collection of the most exact features to form a perfect face. Add to all this a behaviour so full of grace and sweetness, such easy motions with an air so majestic, yet free from stiffness or affectation, that I am persuaded could she be suddenly transported upon the most polite throne of Europe, no body would think her other than born and bred to be a Queen, though educated in a country we call barbarous. To say all in a word, our most celebrated English beauties would vanish near her.

She was dressed in a Caftan of gold brocade, flowered with silver, very well fitted to her shape, and shewing to admiration the beauty of her bosom, only shaded by the thin gauze of her shift. Her drawers were pale pink, her waistcoat green and silver, her slippers white sattin, finely embroidered; her lovely arms adorned with bracelets of diamonds, and her broad girdle set round with diamonds; upon her head a rich Turkish handkerchief of pink and silver, her own fine black hair hanging a great length, in various tresses, and on one side of her head some bodkins of jewels. I am afraid you will accuse me of extravagance in this description. I think I have read some where, that women always speak in rapture, when they speak of beauty, and I cannot imagine why they should not be allowed to do so. I rather think it a virtue to be able to admire without any mixture of desire or envy. The gravest writers have spoke with great warmth of some celebrated pictures and statues. The workmanship of heaven certainly excels all our weak imitations, and, I think, has a much better claim to our praise. For my part, I am not ashamed to own, I took more pleasure in looking on the

beauteous

beauteous Fatima, than the finest piece of sculpture could have given me. She told me the two girls at her feet were her daughters, though she appeared too young to be their mother. Here fair maids were ranged below the Sofa, to the number of twenty, and put me in mind of the pictures of the antient nymphs. I did not think all nature could have furnished such a scene of beauty. She made them a sign to play and dance. Four of them immediately begun to play some soft airs on instruments between a lute and a guitar, which they accompanied with their voices, while the others danced by turns. This dance was very different from what I had seen before. Nothing could be more artful, or more proper to raise *certain ideas.* The tunes so soft;——The motions so languishing?—Accompanied with pauses and dying eyes!—half falling back, and then recovering themselves in so artful a manner, that I am very positive, the coldest and most rigid prude upon earth, could not have looked upon them without thinking of

" something

"something not to be spoke of."—I suppose you may have read that the Turks have no music, but what is shocking to the ears; but this account is from those who never heard any but what is played in the streets, and is just as reasonable, as if a foreigner should take his ideas of English music from the bladder and string, or the marrow-bones and cleavers. I can assure you, that the music is extremely pathetic; 'tis true I am inclined to prefer the Italian, but perhaps I am partial. I am acquainted with a Greek lady, who sings better than Mrs. Robinson; and is very well skilled, in both, who gives the preference to the Turkish. 'Tis certain they have very fine natural voices, these were very agreeable. When the dance was over, four fair slaves came into the room, with silver censors in their hands, and perfumed the air with amber, aloes-wood, and other scents. After this, they served me coffee upon their knees, in the finest Japan china, with *soucoups* of silver gilt. The lovely Fatima entertained me all
this

this while in the moſt polite agreeable manner, calling me often *Uzelle Sultanam*, or the beautiful Sultana, and deſiring my friendſhip with the beſt grace in the world, lamenting that ſhe could not entertain me in my own language.

When I took my leave, two maids brought in a fine ſilver baſket of embroidered handkerchiefs; ſhe begg'd I would wear the richeſt for her ſake, and gave the others to my woman and interpretefs.—I retired, through the ſame ceremonies as before, and could not help thinking I had been ſome time in Mahomet's paradiſe, ſo much was I charmed with what I had ſeen. I know not how the relation of it appears to you. I wiſh it may give you part of my pleaſure; for I would have my dear ſiſter ſhare in all the diverſions of,

Your's, &c.&c.

LETTER XXXIV.

To the Abbot of ———.

Adrianople, May 17, O. S.

I AM going to leave Adrianople, and I would not do it, without giving you some account of all that is curious in it, which I have taken a great deal of pains to see. I will not trouble you with wife differtations, whether or no this is the same city, that was anciently called Orestesit or Oreste, which you know better than I do. It is now called from the Emperor Adrian, and was the first European seat of the Turkish Empire, and has been the favourite residence of many Sultans. MAHOMET the fourth, and MUSTAPHA, the brother of the reigning Emperor, were so fond of it, that they wholly abandoned Constantinople, which humour so far exasperated the Janizaries, that it was a considerable motive to the rebellions that deposed them. Yet this man seems to love to keep his court here,

I can

I can give you no reason for this partiality. 'Tis true, the situation is fine, and the country all round very beautiful; but the air is extremely bad, and the Seraglio itself is not free from the ill effect of it. The town is said to be eight miles in compass, I suppose they reckon in the gardens. There are some good houses in it, I mean large ones; for the architecture of their palaces never makes any great shew. It is now very full of people; but they are most of them such as follow the court, or camp, and when they are removed, I am told 'tis no populous city. The river Maritza (anciently the Hebrus) on which it is situated, is dried up every summer, which contributes very much to make it unwholesome. It is now a very pleasant stream. There are two noble bridges built over it. I had the curiosity to go to see the Exchange in my Turkish dress, which is disguise sufficient. Yet I own, I was not very easy when I saw it crowded with Janizaries; but they dare not be rude to a woman, and made way for me with as much

respect,

respect, as if I had been in my own figure. It is half a mile in length, the roof arched, and kept extremely neat. It holds three hundred and sixty-five shops, furnished with all sorts of rich goods expofed to fale in the fame manner as at the New Exchange in London, but the pavement is kept much neater, and the shops are all fo clean, they feem juſt new painted.— Idle people of all forts walk here for their diverfion, or amufe themfelves with drinking coffee, or sherbet, which is cried about as oranges and fweet-meats are in our playhoufes. I obferved moſt of the rich tradefmen were Jews. That people are in incredible power in this country. They have many privileges above all the natural Turks themfelves, and have formed a very confiderable commonwealth here, being judged by their own laws. They have drawn the whole trade of the Empire into their hands, partly by the firm union amongſt themfelves, and partly by the idle temper and want of induſtry in the Turks. Every Baſſa has his Jew, who is his " *homme* " *d'affaires* ;"

"*d'affaires;*" he is let into all his secrets, and does all his business. No bargain is made, no bribe received, no merchandise disposed of, but what passes through their hands. They are the physicians, the stewards, and the interpreters of all the great men. You may judge how advantageous this is to a people who never fail to make use of the smallest advantages. They have found the secret of making themselves so necessary, that they are certain of the protection of the court, whatever ministry is in power. Even the English, French, and Italian merchants, who are sensible of their artifices, are, however, forced to trust their affairs to their negotiation, nothing of trade being managed without them, and the meanest amongst them being too important to be disobliged, since the whole body take care of his interests with as much vigour as they would those of the most considerable of their members. They are many of them vastly rich, but they take care to make little public shew of it; though they live in their houses in

the

the utmoſt luxury and magnificence. This copious ſubject has drawn me from my deſcription of the exchange, founded by Ali Baſſa, whoſe name it bears. Near it is the Sherſki, a ſtreet of a mile in length, full of ſhops of all kind of fine merchandize, but exceſſive dear, nothing being made here. It is covered on the top with boards to keep out the rain, that merchants may meet conveniently in all weathers. The Beſiten near it, is another exchange, built upon pillars, where all ſorts of horſe furniture are ſold. Glittering every where with gold, rich embroidery and jewels, it makes a very agreeable ſhew. From this place I went in my Turkiſh coach, to the camp, which is to move in a few days to the frontiers. The Sultan is already gone to his tents, and all his court; the appearance of them is indeed, very magnificent. Thoſe of the great men are rather like palaces than tents, taking up a great compaſs of ground, and being divided into a vaſt number of apartments. They are all of green, and the Baſſas of three Tails, have

thoſe

those ensigns of their power placed in a very conspicuous manner before their tents, which are adorned on the top with gilded balls, more or less, according to their different ranks. The ladies go in coaches to see the camp, as eagerly as ours did to that of Hyde Park; but 'tis very easy to observe, that the soldiers do not begin the campaign with any great chearfulness. The war is a general grievance upon the people, but particularly hard upon the tradesmen, now that the Grand Signior is resolved to lead his army in person. Every company of them is obliged, upon this occasion, to make a present according to their ability.

I took the pains of rising at six in the morning to see the ceremony, which did not however begin till eight. The Grand Signior was at the Seraglio window, to see the procession, which passed through the principal streets. It was preceded by an Effendi, mounted on a camel, richly furnished, reading aloud the Alcoran, finely bound, laid upon a cushion. He was surrounded by a parcel of boys, in white, singing

singing some verses of it, followed by a man dressed in green boughs, representing a clean husbandman sowing seed. After him several reapers with garlands of ears of corn, as Ceres is pictured, with scythes in their hands seeming to mow. Then a little machine drawn by oxen, in which was a wind-mill, and boys employed in grinding corn, followed by another machine, drawn by buffaloes carrying an oven, and two more boys, one employed in kneading the bread, and another in drawing it out of the oven. These boys threw little cakes on both sides amongst the crowd, and were followed by the whole company of bakers marching on foot, two by two, in their best clothes, with cakes, loaves, pasties and pies of all sorts on their heads, and after them two buffoons or jack-puddings, with their faces and clothes smeared with meal, who diverted the mob with their antic gestures. In the same manner followed all the companies of trade in the Empire; the nobler sort, such as jewellers, mercers, &c. finely mounted, and many of the pageants

geants that reprefent their trades, perfectly magnificent; amongft which that of the Furriers made one of the beft figures, being a very large machine fet round with the fkins of ermines, foxes, &c. fo well ftuffed, that the animals feemed to be alive, and followed by mufic and dancers. I believe they were, upon the whole, twenty thoufand men, all ready to follow his Highnefs if he commanded them. The rear was clofed by the volunteers, who came to beg the honour of dying in his fervice. This prrt of the fhew feemed to me fo barbarous, that I removed from the window upon the firft appearance of it. They were all naked to the middle. Some had their arms pierced through with arrows left fticking in them. Others had them fticking in their heads, the blood trickling down their faces, Some flafhed their arms with fharp knives, making the blood fpring out upon thofe that ftood there; and this is looked upon as an expreffion of their zeal for glory. I am told, that fome make ufe of it to advance their love;

and

and when they are near the window, where their mistress stands (all the women in town being veiled to see this spectacle) they stick another arrow for her sake, who gives some sign of approbation and encouragement to this gallantry. The whole shew lasted for near eight hours, to my great sorrow, who was heartily tired, though I was in the house of the widow of the Captain Bassa (Admiral) who refreshed me with coffee, sweat-meats, sherbet, &c. with all possible civility.

I went two days after to see the Mosque of Sultan Selim I. which is a building very well worth the curiosity of a traveller. I was dressed in my Turkish habit, and admitted without scruple; though I believe they guessed who I was, by the extreme officiousness of the door keeper, to shew me every part of it. It is situated very advantageously in the midst of the city, and in the highest part of it, making a very noble shew. The first court has four gates, and the innermost three. They are both of them surrounded with cloisters, with marble

marble pillars of the Ionic order finely polished, and of very lively colours, the whole pavement is of white marble, and the roof of the cloisters divided into several cupolas or domes, headed with gilt balls on the top. In the midst of each court are fine fountains of white marble; and before the great gate of the Mosque, a portico with green marble pillars, which has five gates, the body of the Mosque being one prodigious dome. I understand so little of architecture, I dare not pretend to speak of the proportions. It seemed to be very regular; this I am sure of, it is vastly high, and I thought it the noblest building I ever saw. It has two rows of marble galleries on pillars, with marble balustres; the pavement is also covered with Persian carpets. In my opinion, it is a great addition to its beauty, that it is not divided into pews, and encumbered with forms and benches like our churches; nor the pillars (which are most of them red and white marble) disfigured by the little tawdry images and pictures, that give Roman Catholic

tholic churches the air of toy-shops. The walls seemed to be inlaid, with such very lively colours, in small flowers, that I could not imagine what stones had been made use of. But going near, I saw they were crusted with japan china, which has a very beautiful effect. In the midst hung a vast lamp of silver gilt; besides which I do verily believe, there was at least two thousand of a lesser size. This must look very glorious when they are all lighted; but being at night, no women are suffered to enter. Under the large lamp is a great pulpit of carved wood gilt, and just by, a fountain to wash, which you know is an essential part of their devotion. In one corner is a little gallery enclosed with gilded lattices for the Grand Signior. At the upper end a large niche, very like an altar, raised two steps, covered with gold brocade, and standing before it two silver gilt candlesticks, the height of a man, and in them white wax candles as thick as a man's wrist. The outside of the Mosque is adorned with towers vastly high, gilt on the top, from whence

whence the Imaums call the people to prayers. I had the curiosity to go up one of them, which is contrived so artfully, as to give surprize to all that see it. There is but one door, which leads to three different stair-cases, going to the three different stories of the tower, in such a manner, that three priests may ascend, rounding, without ever meeting each other; a contrivance very much admired. Behind the Mosque is an Exchange full of shops, where poor artificers are lodged gratis. I saw several Dervises at their prayers here. They are dressed in a plain piece of woollen, with their arms bare, and a woollen cap on their heads, like a high crowned hat without brims. I went to see some other Mosques, built much after the same manner, but not comparable, in point of magnificence, to this I have described, which is infinitely beyond any church in Germany or England; I won't talk of other countries I have not seen. The Seraglio does not seem a very magnificent palace. But the gardens are very large, plentifully supplied with water,

water, and full of trees; which is all I know of them, having never been in them.

I tell you nothing of the order of Mr. W——'s entry, and his audience. These things are always the same, and have been so often described, I won't trouble you with the repetition. The young Prince, about eleven years old, sits near his father when he gives audience; he is a handsome boy, but probably will not immediately succeed the Sultan, there being two sons of Sultan MUSTAPHA (his eldest brother) remaining; the eldest about twenty years old, on whom the hopes of the people are fixed. This reign has been bloody and avaritious. I am apt to believe they are very impatient to see the end of it. I am, Sir,

Your's, &c. &c.

P. S. I will write to you again from Constantinople.

LETTERS

OF THE RIGHT HONOURABLE

Lady M——y W————y M————e.

Vol. I.

ADVERTISEMENT

OF THE

EDITOR.

THE editor of these Letters, who during his residence at Venice, was honoured with the esteem and friendship of their ingenious and elegant author, presents them to the publick, for the two following reasons:

First, Because it was the manifest intention of the late Lady M—y W——y M——e, that this SELECT COLLECTION of her Letters should be communicated to the public; an intention declared not only to the Editor, but to a few more chosen friends, to whom she gave copies of these incomparable Letters.

The second and principal reason that has engaged the editor to let this collection see the light, is, that the publication of these letters will be an immortal monument to the memory of Lady M——y W——y; and will shew, as long as the English language endures, the sprightliness of her wit, the solidity of her judgment, the extent of her knowledge, the elegance of her taste, and the excellence of her real character.

The

ADVERTISEMENT.

The SELECT COLLECTION, here published, was faithfully transcribed from the original manuscript of her ladyship at Venice.

The Letters from *Ratisbon*, *Vienna*, *Dresden*, *Peterwaradin*, *Belgrade*, *Adrianople*, *Constantinople*, *Pera*, *Tunis*, *Genoa*, *Lyons* and *Paris*, are, certainly, the most curious and interesting part of this publication, and both in point of *matter* and *form*, are, to say no more of them, singularly worthy of the curiosity and attention of all *men of taste*, and even of all *women of fashion*. As to those female readers, who read for improvement, and think their beauty an insipid thing, if it is not seasoned by intellectual charms, they will find in these Letters what they seek for, and will behold in their author, an ornament and model to their sex.

LETTER XXXV.

To the Abbot ———.

Constantinople, May 29, O. S.

I HAVE had the advantage of very fine weather all my journey, and as the summer is now in its beauty, I enjoyed the pleasure of fine prospects; and the meadows being full of all sorts of garden flowers, and sweet herbs, my berlin perfumed the air as it pressed them. The Grand Signior furnished us with thirty covered waggons for our baggage, and five coaches of the country for my women. We found the road full of the great Spahis and their equipages coming out of Asia to the war. They always travel with tents; but I chose to lie in houses all the way. I will not trouble you with the names of the villages we passed, in which there was nothing remarkable, but at Ciorlei, where there was a Conac, or little Seraglio, built for the use of the Grand Signior, when he goes this road. I had the curiosity

osity to view all the apartments destined for the ladies of his court. They were in the midst of a thick grove of trees, made fresh by fountains: but I was most surprised to see the walls almost covered with little distichs of Turkish verse, writ with pencils. I made my interpreter explain them to me, and I found several of them very well turned; though I easily believed him, that they had lost much of their beauty in the translation. One was literally thus in English:

We come into this world; we lodge and we depart;
He never goes that ledg'd within my heart.

The rest of our journey was through fine painted meadows, by the side of the sea of Marmora, the ancient Propontis. We lay the next night at Selivrea, anciently a noble town. —It is now a good sea-port, and neatly built enough, and has a bridge of thirty-two arches. Here is a famous ancient Greek church.——I had given one of my coaches to a Greek lady, who desired the conveniency of travelling with me;

me; she designed to pay her devotions, and I was glad of the opportunity of going with her. I found it an ill-built edifice, set out with the same sort of ornaments, but less rich, as the Roman Catholic churches. They shewed me a saint's body, where I threw a piece of money; and a picture of the Virgin Mary, drawn by the hand of St. Luke, very little to the credit of his painting; but, however, the finest Madona of Italy is not more famous for her miracles. The Greeks have a monstrous taste in their pictures, which, for more finery, are always drawn upon a gold ground. You may imagine what a good air this has; but they have no notion either of shade or proportion. They have a bishop here, who officiated in his purple robe, and sent me a candle almost as big as myself for a present, when I was at my lodging. We lay that night at a town called Bujuk Cekmege, or Great Bridge; and the night following at Kujuk Cekmege, or Little Bridge, in a very pleasant lodging, formerly a monastery of Dervises, having before it a large court, encompassed with marble cloisters, with a good fountain in the middle. The prospect from this place, and the gardens round it, is the most agreeable I have seen; and shews, that monks of all religions know how to chuse their retirements. 'Tis now belonging to a Hogia, or school-master, who teaches boys here. I asked him to shew me his own apartment, and was surprised to see him point to a tall cypress tree in the garden, on the top of which was a place for a bed for himself, and a little lower, one for his wife and two children, who slept there every night. I was so much diverted with the fancy, I resolved to examine his nest nearer, but after going up fifty steps, I found I had still fifty to go up, and then I must climb from branch to branch, with some hazard of my neck, I thought it therefore the best way to come down again.

We arrived the next day at Constantinople; but I can yet tell you very little of it, all my time having been taken up with receiving visits, which are, at least, a very good entertainment

to

to the eyes, the young women being all beauties, and their beauty highly improved by the high taste of their dress. Our palace is in Pera, which is no more a suburb of Constantinople, than Westminster is a suburb to London. All the Ambassadors are lodged very near each other. One part of our house shews us the Port, the City, and the Seraglio, and the distant hills of Asia; perhaps, all together, the most beautiful prospect in the world.

A certain French author says, Constantinople is twice as big as Paris. Mr. W——y is unwilling to own 'tis bigger than London, though I confess it appears to me to be so; but I don't believe 'tis so populous. The burying fields about it, are certainly much larger than the whole city. 'Tis surprizing what a vast deal of land is lost this way in Turkey. Sometimes I have seen burying places of several miles, belonging to very inconsiderable villages, which were formerly great towns, and retain no other mark of their antient grandeur, than this dismal one. On no occasion do they ever remove

remove a stone that serves for a monument. Some of them are costly enough, being of very fine marble. They set up a pillar with a carved turbant on the top of it to the memory of a man; and as the turbants, by their different shapes, shew the quality or profession, 'tis in a manner putting up the arms of the deceased. Besides, the pillar commonly bears an inscription in gold letters. The ladies have a simple pillar, without other ornament, except those that die unmarried, who have a rose on the top of their monument. The sepulchres of particular families are railed in, and planted round with trees. Those of the Sultans, and some great men, have lamps constantly burning in them.

When I spoke of their religion, I forgot to mention two particularities, one of which I had read of, but it seemed so odd to me, I could not believe it; yet 'tis certainly true; that when a man has divorced his wife, in the most solemn manner, he can take her again upon no other terms, than permitting another man to pass a night with her; and there are

some

some examples of those, who have submitted to this law, rather than not have back their beloved. The other point of doctrine is very extraordinary. Any woman that dies unmarried, is looked upon to die in a state of reprobation. To confirm this belief, they reason, that the end of the creation of woman, is to increase and multiply, and that she is only properly employed in the works of her calling, when she is bringing forth children, or taking care of them, which are all the virtues that God expects from her. And indeed their way of life, which shuts them out of all public commerce, does not permit them any other.— Our vulgar notion, that they don't own women to have any souls, is a mistake. 'Tis true they say, they are not of so elevated a kind, and therefore must not hope to be admitted into the Paradise appointed for the men, who are to be entertained by celestial beauties. But there is a place of happiness destined for souls of the inferior order, where all good women are to be in eternal bliss. Many of them are

are very superstitious, and will not remain widows ten days, for fear of dying in the reprobate state of a useless creature. But those that like their liberty, and are not slaves to their religion, content themselves with marrying when they are afraid of dying. This is a piece of theology very different from that which teaches nothing to be more acceptable to God, than a vow of perpetual virginity: which divinity is most rational, I leave you to determine.

I have already made some progress in a collection of Greek medals. Here are several professed antiquaries, who are ready to serve any body that desires them. But you cannot imagine how they stare in my face, when I enquire about them, as if nobody was permitted to seek after medals, till they were grown a piece of antiquity themselves. I have got some very valuable ones of the Macedonian Kings, particularly one of Perseus, so lively, I fancy I can see all his ill qualities in his face. I have a Porphyry head finely cut, of the true Greek sculpture;

sculpture; but who it represents, is to be guessed at by the learned when I return. For you are not to suppose these antiquaries (who are all Greeks) know any thing. Their trade is only to sell; they have correspondents at Aleppo, Grand Cairo, in Arabia and Palestine, who send them all they can find, and very often great heaps, that are only fit to melt into pans and kettles. They get the best price they can for any of them, without knowing those that are valuable, from those that are not. Those that pretend to skill, generally find out the image of some Saint in the medals of the Greek cities. One of them, shewing me the figure of a Pallas, with a victory in her hand on a reverse, assured me, it was the Virgin holding a crucifix. The same man offered me the head of a Socrates, on a Sardonix; and, to enhance the value, give him the title of Saint Augustin. I have bespoke a mummy, which, I hope, will come safe to my hands, notwithstanding the misfortune that befel a very fine one, designed for the King of Sweden. He

gave

gave a great price for it, and the Turks took it into their heads, that he muſt have ſome conſiderable project depending upon it. They fancied it the body of God knows who, and that the ſtate of their empire myſtically depended on the conſervation of it. Some old prophecies were remembered upon this occaſion, and the mummy committed priſoner to the Seven Towers, where it has remained under cloſe confinement ever ſince. I dare not try my intereſt in ſo conſiderable a point, as the releaſe of it; but I hope mine will paſs without examination.—I can tell you nothing more at preſent of this famous city. When I have looked a little about me, you ſhall hear from me again. I am, Sir,

Your's, &c. &c.

End of the Firſt Volume.

www.ingramcontent.com/pod-product-compliance
Lightning Source LLC
Chambersburg PA
CBHW021819230426
43669CB00008B/800